Nobody's Hero

Second edition, published in 2001 by

WOODFIELD PUBLISHING
Bognor Regis, West Sussex PO21 5EL, England.

ISBN 1-873203-38-1

Nobody's Hero

Misadventures of an
RAF Policeman in World War II

BERNARD
HART-HALLAM

Woodfield Publishing
WEST SUSSEX ~ ENGLAND

*I dedicate this book
to my dear wife
Jeanette (née Toledo)*

Lt General Von Briesen takes the salute at the triumphant Nazi march past in Paris 1940.

The very first British jet-propelled aircraft, The Gloster Whittle E28/39 on the apron at RAF Shennington, near Banbury, Oxon. The Gloster and Power Jets engineers are preparing the machine for an engine test firing operation. The Gloster Aircraft Company designed and bult the aircraft. Power Jets Ltd invented and built the engine (see chapter 6).

NOBODY'S HERO

Contents

In the period following the ceasefire, a state of 'non-fraternisation' existed (but proved difficult to maintain). We had our own money, printed in note form and designated "British Armed Forces Special Vouchers". The notes were denominated as sixpence, one shilling, five shillings and one pound.

The notes were valid only for transactions within official canteens and organisations. We were not permitted to transfer them to any person not entitled to use British Service Canteens.. Improper use rendered the offender liable to prosecution. (See Chapter 14.)

Preface

The following chapters are an account of my experiences during the period 1941-1946. They include the factual, the absurd, the bizarre, the humorous and the dangerous events in which I became involved. Part of it – as a non-combatant's account of life in the front line of an overseas war zone – may be considered unique. I believe the succeeding chapters may support this point of view.

The PM Branch played a vital part in wartime operations, particularly on foreign soil, where it was continually faced with problems not readily resolvable as a result of previous training or experience.

When the land assault on Hitler's Fortress Europe (code name Operation Overlord) began on D-Day, 6th June 1944, I was the first RAF man to set foot on the Normandy Beach. This was later confirmed to me by the Naval Beach Commander on 'Juno' Beach where my Section landed at around 9am. The Infantry assault on "Juno" Beach had begun just before 8am.

My Section followed this by being the first RAF Unit to enter Belgium, Holland and Germany. A creditworthy treble for a Section classified as 'non-combatants'.

In the latter days of the war I arrested a German Army General and claim to be the only member of the Royal Air Force ever to have done so! I also took part in the liberation of Denmark in 1945.

Writing this account of my wartime service after an interval of over fifty years has presented me with problems due mainly to the fact that I have had to rely on a memory. The details I have committed to print are as accurate as I can recall. I had no personal records on which to draw.

Bernard Hart-Hallam, 2001

Publisher's Note: In 1994 and 1995 Bernard Hart-Hallam was decorated by the French, Dutch & Danish Governments in recognition of his service from D-Day onwards.

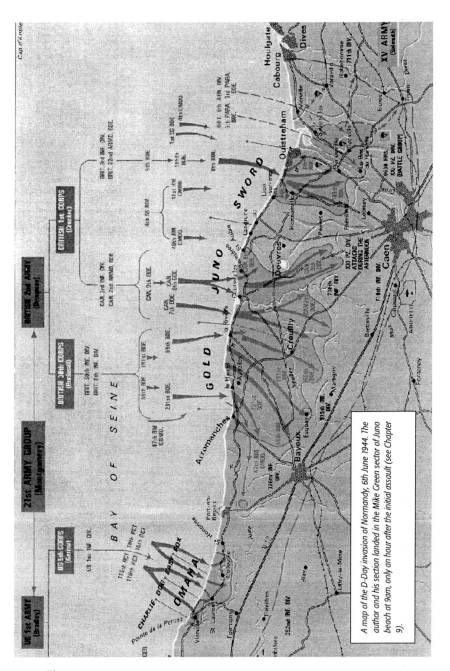

A map of the D-Day invasion of Normandy, 6th June 1944. The author and his section landed in the Mike Green sector of Juno beach at 9am, only an hour after the initial assault (see Chapter 9).

NOBODY'S HERO

Acknowledgements

I wish to thank the following for their invaluable help in preparing the manuscript:

My brother Arnold of Shirebrook, Near Mansfield, Notts.

Mary and Alison Rowland of Leighton Buzzard.

Staff at Leighton Buzzard Library - Anne Howard and Marjorie Grant, in particular.

Peter Stowe - formerly Headmaster - Cedars School, Leighton Buzzard

My daughter, Laura Layton, at Leighton Buzzard.

The Royal Air Force Museum.

The Martin Baker Aircraft Company.

The author after completing his RAF Police training, 1941.

CHAPTER ONE

Joining up

Enlisting in the Armed Forces at the beginning of the 1939-45 War was relatively straightforward. There were recruiting stations in most towns in the United Kingdom, and all one had to do was to present oneself at one of them and state one's intentions. Mine had always been to join the Royal Air Force. Providing one was fit and well and below the age of 45, acceptance was almost automatic. I was born near the RAF Station at Hucknall and the aerodrome had played a background part in the lives of my family. I suppose this had to have a bearing on my choice of service. I went to my first flying display at the age of five, with my Father. The year was 1925.

At the time when war broke out I was serving a two year probation period in the Police force, and this meant that I was not liable for "call-up' even though I was of an age that made me a prime candidate for conscription into the Armed Forces. Certain occupations had been classified by the Government as essential to the War effort, and this meant that the individuals so classified were automatically exempted from Service in the Armed Forces. The Police Force came into this category – at least for the early part of the War; the official term used was a "Reserved Occupation".

I soon came to realise, however, that being in a reserved occupation when most young men had already been conscripted into the Armed Forces, made life hard to cope with, particularly as I was frequently being forcibly told by members of the public that I should be off fighting for my country like other boys. I did my best to cope with these jibes, but I eventually managed to obtain my release, early in 1941, and this came as something of a relief.

From 1941 onwards the recruitment of part-time Special Constables enabled more and more regular policemen to volunteer for War Service with the Armed Forces.

I duly presented myself at a recruiting station located in a public swimming bath in the town of Mansfield. There were three desks on view, in line abreast, and seated at each of the three were Recruiting Officers representing the Army, the Royal Navy and the Royal Air Force.

An Army Sergeant was in charge of the reception arrangements and after eyeing me up and down he suggested that I was the right height and build for the Brigade of Guards. I said 'no' to this. He then suggested that the Navy were keen to recruit young men as Stokers, but I again said no. He then directed me to the RAF desk where I was interviewed and finally enlisted in the Royal Air Force Volunteer Reserve. My allocated branch, the RAF Police, was a constituent part of the RAF Provost Marshal's organisation (Referred to hereafter as the PM Branch) and logically, this followed from my former occupation.

I returned home feeling quite pleased, and my call-up papers arrived within days. I was provided with a Railway Travel Warrant, some minor instructions, and, in due course, I reported to the main Guardroom at the RAF Station at Padgate, near Manchester, complete with suitcase, pyjamas, toothbrush, shaving kit and the clothes I stood up in. The date was 28th April, 1941 – my twenty-first birthday.

CHAPTER TWO

Induction at RAF Padgate

To many RAF personnel the name Padgate was synonymous with the process by which men and women who had volunteered, or had been conscripted for service with the Royal Air Force, were inducted straight from civilian life. Padgate was a major establishment where thousands of new recruits were inducted in a very short space of time; the Service was expanding at a very substantial rate and the demand for additional men and women for the War effort was considerable.

I suppose, if I am honest, my short stay at Padgate represented the kind of cultural shock that I found hard to live with. The bulk of those individuals exercising direct authority over me had been pre-war members of the RAF, and during the early part of the War they had been given rank and authority for the first time in their lives. They seemed to predominate as Non-Commissioned Officers (NCOs) at Corporal and Sergeant level, and it was evident that they had had precious little training in the business of controlling men. As a generalisation this was how I found them, but here and there were the welcome exceptions. I had been used to the effects of rank in the Police Service and this helped me to tolerate some of the excesses of the below-standard NCOs.

On the day of arrival, along with other recruits, I was allocated a place in a barrack hut housing thirty men in total. The hut contained a number of two-tier bunk beds on either side of a central gangway, with a separate NCOs room at one end. Each bed had a mattress, four blankets and a pillow. Each bed space had a locker for each recruit's use. The washing and lavatory facilities were in a separate building nearby. There was no hot water. These buildings were commonly known as "The Ablutions".

The other twenty-nine occupants of the hut were from different walks of life and places of origin and it followed that they were of different ages, shapes, sizes and temperaments. At one stage I could not help thinking that I was back in the Boy Scouts attending Camp with a group of individuals whom I had never met before. It certainly seemed unreal, but the harsh facts of life in an armed service in wartime soon dispelled any notions that we were there to have a good time.

As the days passed we got to talking to each other about what we had been doing in civilian life and, to me, coming as I had from a tightly knit coal mining community, some of the information that came out was both interesting and revealing; some of it was a good deal less than this. Some of our number exercised their right to say nothing, and they usually remained aloof as much as was possible within the confines of a barrack hut. As to the bunk beds, I took the top one because, being of above average height, climbing up there was relatively easy. Another Airman took the bottom bunk. He was of no more than medium height so we were a bit of a contrast, physically.

I soon came to realise that my bunk-mate and I were from very different backgrounds. He had had a Public School and University education and mine had been a good deal less distinguished. His speech was polished and precise, and the way in which he comported himself, in general, demonstrated that he was probably a 'somebody'. After a couple of days I found myself totally relaxed in his company, and that pleased me no end. We were probably about the same age.

The fact that he had money to spend also had the effect of singling him out from the rest of the hut's inmates. The majority of us were more or less dependent on the small wage the RAF paid us, but he was able, and willing, to buy rounds of beer in the Canteen and thought nothing of it. My weekly wage for quite some time was ten shillings, at a time when the average wage outside the Armed Forces was somewhere between four and five pounds a week.

We used Christian names nearly all the time, so it was not particularly important to know someone else's surname. In the case of my bunkmate I had noticed the name "Colman" on his shaving kit, and he told me he came from Norwich. We continued to get on well together and when he obtained a Weekend Leave Pass I walked with him on the Friday afternoon to the main Camp exit. Waiting there was a Rolls Royce motor car, chauffeur-driven, with a lady sitting in the back. Colman climbed into the Rolls, kissed the lady on the cheek, and the car drove away. I was little short of flabbergasted and certainly intrigued.

When Colman came back on the Sunday night I resisted the temptation to ask him the question uppermost in my mind. Instead I made the assumption, possibly quite erroneously, that he was one of the famous 'mustard' Colmans of Norfolk.

Another hut mate seemed to spend most of his time boasting and showing off photographs of his house and its obviously lavish contents, which, as a Conscript, he had probably been reluctant to leave. He was a proper show off, but he kind of got his comeuppance when someone revealed that he was a market trader in fruit and vegetables and not the business executive he was trying to pass himself off as. But to be fair to him his description of himself as being "in food" was accurate!

A third character deserves a mention. He was in his late twenties and a marvellous physical specimen of a man: six feet tall, muscular and disgustingly athletic. He smiled the moment you looked at him and obviously he was everybody's friend. He said his name was "Oggie", he maintained that he did not have another name, but days later we learned that he answered to the tag of 'Aircraftsman Smith'. He was proud of having had 'no fixed abode' apart from a garden shed on an allotment at Ossett in Yorkshire. Another of his boasts was that they had had to burn the primary school down to get him out of Class Two! The buzz was that he could neither read nor write. But he was certainly interesting.

Among the remainder, there was an undergraduate, a shopkeeper, a mechanic, a male nurse, a teacher, a plumber and a musician.

It soon became more than obvious that it took all kinds to make up an intake such as we were.

On Day One we were documented and left to settle in. The high spot of being documented was receiving my rank, Aircraftsman 2nd Class, and my personal Service Number, 1528102, which stayed with me through to demobilisation. The frequent use of the last three digits of this number became an ingrained feature of service life and woe betide the Airman who could not trot them out like a parrot. The kind of service number allocated also had a substantial element of "one-upmanship" in it, and as mine happened to be in excess of one and a half million, I came in for a fair amount of stick.

At the onset I had no idea that the length of time one had been in the Service was of such importance to others and the moment I trotted out my 1528102 there were loud cries of "Get some in", meaning "Get some Service in". An Airman with a number under a million behaved as though it was the equivalent of some sort of decoration for services rendered. The accent on one's number was such that on one occasion two Airmen actually got to blows!

Documentation also resulted in my being issued with two identity discs on a length of cord sufficient to enable them to be draped necklace fashion around the neck. One disc was said to be fireproof and the other one rot proof. The disc bore my name and Service Number. I wore them solidly for five years.

I was also issued with two gold lapel badges bearing the letters "VR". This was short for Volunteer Reserve★ and as the words indicate the badges were issued to show that one was a Volunteer and not a Conscript. I wore these badges for some time, but on occasion they became a matter for contention when one was among Conscripts so I discontinued the practice of wearing them. Oaths of loyalty to King and Country were also taken.

★**Author's Note:** The RAF Volunteer Reserve was formed in the 1930s to provide a reserve of airmen in case of need. A Special VR tie is worn today by former members of this branch of the Services.

NOBODY'S HERO

On Day Two I was kitted out with RAF uniform and the procedure for this was both enlightening and interesting. All new recruits were paraded crocodile fashion at a Stores Unit building which in civilian life would have been described as a Warehouse. The queue was about a hundred deep and when my turn came, I found myself at a counter about forty feet long. The various items making up a uniform were allocated at specific points along the counter and allocations were made by NCOs from behind the counter. For shoes and shirts the procedure was logical because I was able to give my foot and neck sizes, but for most of the other items, the judgement of the NCO behind the counter was paramount. He decided what to issue to you by the process of looking you up and down. In cases of doubt, the views of a Senior NCO, who patrolled in the background, were obtained. His word was law. I feared the worst from the start being six foot four inches tall with an arm span of six feet eight inches. I was at the counter for about ten minutes all told achieving my allocation. The basic wardrobe was a cap, three shirts, three vests, three pants, three pairs of socks, two pairs of trousers, one battle dress blouse, one dress tunic, one greatcoat, one tie, one pair of boots, one pair of braces, two towels and one canvas kit bag. I returned to the barrack block and tried on the various items of uniform and contrary to my expectations found that they were a fairly good fit; there was obviously more skill employed by the issuers than I had thought possible.

Again, somewhat to my surprise, I found that the other occupants of the block had had similar experiences and I could not remember anyone having to go back to the Stores for a refit. The kit-bag was made of tough canvas, cylindrical in shape and was the only permitted means of containing one's equipment. The open end of the bag was fitted with brass eyelets and a short rope with which to secure the contents. My civilian attire I then packed and despatched to my home at Shirebrook, near Mansfield, Nottinghamshire, at my own expense. From Day Two onwards it was uniform all the way.

On Day Three we were required to be on parade at 8am sharp. Breakfast, which was available from 7am took the form of porridge, eggs or fish, bread, jam and a mug of tea. Most of the fish, large pieces of haddock, went back to the kitchen.

The parade was a simple affair conducted by a young officer named Farr, who someone said was none other than the talented Welsh pugilist who, some years previously had been to the United States of America and fought for the Heavyweight Boxing Championship of the World. His attitude to the new recruits was excellent and he did a lot in a short time to make us feel good in our new environment. We did little else that morning.

Lunch was at 12.30 and the Airmen's mess proved to be a new experience for most of us. The sight of hundreds of men sitting down under one roof at one time almost defied belief. The meal itself was a basic meat and two vegetables course followed by rice pudding and a mug of tea. The standard of the meal was good and the portions were ample. The Orderly Officer's appearance half way through the meal provided a bit of light relief if only for the antics of a Flight-Sergeant who was acting as a kind of escort to the Orderly Officer.

I had never seen nor heard anything quite like him before and it took me all my time to refrain from bursting out laughing. The Flight Sergeant walked in front of the Orderly Officer and at an interval of half dozen or so rows of tables he paused, raised his right knee about waist height then crashed his right foot down on to the concrete with sufficient force to dislocate the average person's leg joints. He followed these antics with the cry of "Horderly Officar!" The Orderly Officer then proceeded to walk past the end of each table enquiring if anyone had any complaints to make about the food. Contrary to expectations, one recruit stood up at the next table to mine and managed to withstand the distinctly hostile glare given him by the Flight Sergeant. The Orderly Officer then spoke to the complaining airman whom I quickly assumed was not keen on being an asset to the Service. His complaint was that he did not eat meat and the rest of the meal was cold, anyway. He was requested to accompany the Orderly Officer to the kitchen serving hatches and this he did, carefully flanked by the Flight Sergeant. I did not hear the outcome, but a wag sitting at a table nearby was heard to say that the complainant was probably on the Flight Sergeant's hit list already - not a very pleasant prospect for a new recruit.

On other days, Senior NCOs and Officers talked to us in groups about various aspects of Service life and I found these meetings both informative and well presented. They certainly gave me confidence. Weekend passes were given to roughly half of our intake, but I stayed in Camp.

I usually spent evenings at the NAAFI (Navy, Army and Air Force Institute) canteen where indoor games, alcohol and other refreshments were available at reasonable prices.

Great emphasis was continually placed on appearance and we were rapidly persuaded into kit-cleaning activities. An average session for this was at least one hour per night, just before we got into bed. Other aspects of kit cleaning included doing one's own laundry, from the washing stage through to and including the ironing. We had been issued with three of all the basic items of clothing so the usual drill was, one set on, one in the wash and one in the locker. Ironing shirts was demanding because the level of inspections carried out on us was severe. Some of the recruits even introduced the sophistication of starching their shirt collars. Pressing trousers and tunics (jackets) had to be done to a high standard and polishing one's boots could take hours. The spit and polish technique on boots had to be embraced quickly, because they came under very positive surveillance by the NCOs who were responsible for individual "squads". The Air Force term for a "squad" was a "flight". The Army's equivalent was a platoon.

I was usually in bed by 10pm when the NCO in charge of our hut came in and put the lights out. Waking up was seldom a problem. No more than half the recruits slept through the whole night, so there was a general awakening from 6am onwards. It also took a while to get used to bunk beds and flock mattresses.

The stay in Padgate came to an end on the fifteenth day when postings for new recruits to other RAF units were announced.

My particular posting took the unexpected form of a train journey to Whitley Bay, a resort on the North-east coast where I and several other recruits were billeted with a seaside Landlady, who was kindness itself. I assumed that there was some deep purpose behind this transfer, but the buzz was that recruits were posted out from Padgate to places like Whitley Bay pending posting to an established RAF Unit. Intake into the RAF at that time appeared to be outstripping the ability of the Administration to cope, or so we thought.

We were paraded and drilled on the promenade once or twice a day to maintain morale, but we were usually back at the billet by 5pm, finished for the day. Initially, drill sessions were a bit of a pantomime, particularly when some recruits demonstrated that they were unable to co-ordinate the swinging of their arms with the forward movement of the legs. It seemed to be the case that in every group of thirty recruits there was at least one who could not avoid taking the left arm and the left leg forward at the same time; some recruits also had great difficulty in keeping in step and they seemed incapable of marching in unison with the rest, try as they may. The solution to both these malfunctions was found in the formation of what became known as "The Awkward Squad". In the Whitley Bay context they numbered about a dozen. Fortunately for them there seemed to be slightly less emphasis on a high standard of drill in the RAF, so the sufferers did not go through the agonies for extended periods of time.

The weather during our time at Whitely Bay was good and being by the sea tended to add to illusion that we were there on holiday; an irksome 9:20pm curfew was in force for recruits, however, every night of the week. One of the highlights of my brief stay at Whitley Bay arose as a direct result of this curfew. One night I found myself sprinting home from a pub in my socks with RAF police NCOs in hot pursuit. I had misjudged the time it would take to get from the pub to my billet and at the curfew time I was running for my life. I made my billet without being arrested, but had I failed to do so my career in the Provost Branch may not have materialised! I never did get to understand the magic of the 9:20 p.m. curfew, but doubtless the RAF had its reasons.

The streets at night were empty and blacked-out as a precaution against air raids, and the sound of an Airman walking or running in service boots carried for a couple of hundred yards. It therefore became accepted practice to walk or run in one's socks so as to avoid detection by the police patrols. The socks were indestructible, anyway, as we were later to find out.

At the end of the second week my posting to RAF Bridgenorth, Shropshire came through. Throughout our time at Whitley Bay our Landlady had treated us like members of her family and this made it something of a sad occasion when I left to start my journey to RAF Bridgenorth. I was probably homesick at the time and not realising it.

CHAPTER THREE

Disciplinary Training at RAF Bridgenorth

Bridgenorth was another major RAF establishment situated on high ground about half an hour's walk from the Town of the same name.

The business of the permanent staff at the Station was to convert recruits into credible, disciplined Servicemen in the quickest possible time. My own intake was said to be made up of seven hundred recruits, designated a Wing. The Wing was sub-divided into a number of Flights of about fifty recruits each. Each Flight was in the charge of a Corporal whose job it was to undertake the bulk of our basic training. There were intermediate RAF Groupings known as Squadrons, but these seemed not to be prominent at basic training units. The buzz was that seven hundred recruits arrived every week and seven hundred departed at the same time, but we had no proof that this was the case.

The programme of training from the day following arrival was both rigorous and demanding. I was billeted in a standard barrack hut with twenty-seven other recruits. A huge solid fuel stove situated in the centre gangway was the only form of heating, but it was effective. We slept on one up one down bunk beds. Bedding included a mattress, a pillow and case and four good quality blankets. A senior NCO occupied a separate room at one end of the hut. In theory, and not much more as things turned out, his job was to ensure that we behaved whilst in the hut and were in bed by "lights out". The washing facilities, housed in a nearby hut, were Spartan compared with average civilian standards. A series of taps were positioned over a lead-lined central trough type sink and the water, which was available in plentiful supply, was cold. The sinks were usable from either side so we washed head to head. The "lavatories" were rows of cubicles providing facilities of the removable tin bucket type and a high standard of cleanliness prevailed. There were shower baths in a separate building, but hot water was not always available. For shaving purposes we provided our own mirrors and cold-water shaving with open razors was less than pleasant. Sore and cut faces were regularly on view. A Rolls self-stropping razor, was definitely a prestige item.

The day began with an early call at 7am. One of our NCO's typical greetings, which he thought was very clever, was "Put 'em away and get out of bed!" First parade was at 8am. Lateness seldom occurred, but when it did it was always punished. Breakfast was from 7am to 8am, but after the first few days I tended to give it a miss. The food was bland and the atmosphere in the dining room was fairly depressing, particularly when haddock was on the menu. The airman in the bunk below mine never went to breakfast. His preference was to prop himself up and smoke a cigarette. He said he could not start the day without one. I estimated his age as early fifties, but he swore he was only 45. He also was a Volunteer and I convinced myself that he had lied about his age. He was obviously delighted at being in the Royal Air Force.

There were two basic training elements that dominated the day's programme and they were foot and rifle drill in squads of 28, on the main square. The rifles were standard issue SMLE (Short Magazine Lee Enfield). We were not issued with ammunition. The Station Headquarters and other Staff Buildings were positioned on three sides of a square, so drill took place in what was almost a box with a tar macadam base. Our appointed Corporal in charge of 'foot drill' wore First World War medal ribbons and was an old soldier in every sense of the term. He was a very firm, but sensible NCO, and in a matter of a few days we were doing our best for him. He knew the tricks of his trade and he put them into practice. Being six feet four inches tall myself I was always his right hand marker or pivot man for foot and rifle drill routines.

Before commencing each drill session, and there was one most mornings to start the day off, he inspected our turnout and he came down hard if he thought we were not putting in the required level of effort with our shoes, buttons and uniform in general. Beards were taboo and he could pick out an unshaven face from feet away. He insisted on short hair and he made a practice each week of despatching individuals to the Camp Barber's Shop for a hair cut, regardless of the true state of their hair. He was always turned out impeccably himself, setting a good example and he was patient when putting us through the various drill movements.

He explained that he was with us for the whole of our stay at Bridgenorth. We were told that this would be eight weeks in total. He also left us in no doubt that when the passing-out parade took place during the eighth week, he expected his squad to be a cut above the rest. He worked us hard and one of his motivating tactics was fascinating. He would march us across the huge square and when our backs were towards the Commanding Officer's office he urged us to do better because "the CO is looking through the window, trying to spot individuals whom he can consider for promotion!" It took us all of a day to come to the realisation that he was using a well-tested confidence trick to make us concentrate on what we were doing and perform to high standards. He kept his distance from the Flight, but he had a sense of humour, which helped us to respect him.

Afternoons were devoted to learning about weapons and firearms followed by the firing of live ammunition at a rifle range. To most of us this was more than interesting if only because for the first time in our lives we were holding a lethal weapon in our hands. We soon discovered that the job of the NCO in charge of the Rifle Range was not without its hazards. One of the recruits firing in the particular detail to which I was allocated managed to put a bullet between the NCO's legs without hitting him. This, of course, was not an acceptable part of the training and the offending recruit was soon made aware of this.

The drill at the range was such that there were fifteen firing platforms opposite fifteen targets. The distance between the two varied but it was usually about fifty yards. We were marched on to the firing positions, from behind, complete with unloaded rifles. Individually, we laid our rifles on the ground parallel with the firing platforms with the nozzle (the business end) pointing towards the target. We then lay flat on our stomachs on the platforms. An NCO moved along the positions and issued each one of us with a clip of bullets, which we fed into the rifle's magazine; we were then addressed by the NCO in charge of the range. He had positioned himself between us and the targets, he stood to attention and his message came out as though it were a gramophone recording. "Bring the weapon up to your shoulder, point it at the target, focus the sights with the tip of the foresight in the centre of the "U" (as in you) and in line with the aperture in the backsight, aim at the lowest central portion of the target which is six o'clock on the bull. Then squeeze the trigger".

The whole message was delivered without a pause and apparently without the taking of a breath. An automaton could not have done it better. The foresight was a metal triangle close to the nozzle end of the gun and the backsight was a metal oblong with an aperture cut into it close to the magazine end. After a while, the advice on how to aim made sense and provided the rifle was kept steady and the trigger was squeezed not snatched, the bullets hit the target. We were then ordered to lay the rifles down and the targets were assessed by the NCO in charge. His verdict was a simple Pass or Fail. Repeat sessions at the range continued until such time as the NCO in charge was satisfied that we were capable of handling and firing a rifle, efficiently and effectively. I found this aspect of our training both absorbing and interesting.

Hand grenade throwing was also an interesting part of the programme. Grenades were about the same size as a cricket ball and they became "live" when one removed a pin which was in place to keep the firing mechanism in a safe mode. The drill was to crouch, usually behind the wall of a sandbag trench, remove the pin, count to four, hurl the grenade at a target twenty to thirty yards away, then duck behind the sandbags. Most grenades exploded, but the odd one did not. When this happened the NCO in charge would climb out of the trench and retrieve the faulty grenade. When

I saw this happen for the first time I was amazed that he was not blown to smithereens. He had obviously carried out this manoeuvre before, but I never understood how he got away with it. The thought did occur though that perhaps the operative at the munitions factory had omitted an essential element when the grenade was assembled. Grenades were mass-produced and mistakes were bound to have occurred.

Handling a rifle with a bayonet affixed was a separate exercise that went on for a number of days. The targets were sacks of straw hung up, in echelon, on frames to represent a row of human bodies. On receipt of the order "charge" ten men in a row were required to yell at the top of their voices, charge a predetermined sack, insert the bayonet and withdraw it in a very specific way, then carry on running until the NCO in charge called a halt. The space between the sacks was narrow and one Airman who got a bit over-excited managed to charge the wrong sack and ended up giving the man next to him a minor back wound. Thereafter, our Corporal was a pains to explain that realism to that extent was not quite what he was expecting or looking for.

One half day each week was designated "Games Afternoon' and almost every conceivable kind of outdoor recreational activity was freely available. We were required to take part in one particular activity or another regardless of the state of our health or the weather. Physical training and ball games sessions took place for periods of up to two hours and were very demanding. Hot showers were available afterwards except when, as occasionally happened, the water was cold. The tea meal on sports day was the best of the week and we usually did it justice. One of the enjoyable menus was French bread, eggs, margarine, cheese, jam in more or less unlimited quantities, and rice pudding for "afters". We usually came away with a full stomach.

A programme of inoculations against various diseases, was carried out, in the mass. On a given day, as many as two to three hundred men were

---

Author's Note: One of our star Physical Training instructors was none other than Jack "Kid" Berg who before the war had fought for a World Boxing title. Jack was the complete extrovert and everybody liked him.

lined up in the open, and if the weather was fine, Medical Officers gave injections sitting at tables outside a barrack hut. The queue moved slowly towards the tables, but not all of the intended "inoculees" got there. I was on two such parades, at intervals, and on both occasions at least half a dozen men fell flat on their faces before they reached the tables. For myself, I made a point of not looking at the Medical Officers doing the inoculations when I came near to the head of the queue. I found this helped. Others succumbed when they saw the needle being shot into someone else's arm.

Some of the inoculations caused me to feel groggy and there was no shortage of advice as to how best to react after being "jabbed". The popular line of advice was that one should exercise the arm as much as possible, but, as often as not, this made one feel a damned sight worse. I settled for sitting next to the stove, keeping warm and keeping still. We were excused parades for two days if we were really off colour. After forty-eight hours most of us were back to normal.

In theory we were allowed out of the Camp during the evening, but getting out via the Guardroom at the main Camp entrance turned out to be an unexpected hazard. I had been content to stay in Camp for the first week or so because I did not fancy the long walk to Bridgenorth and back just to get a beer when I could get one at a NAAFI canteen within the Camp itself. I was persuaded, however, to join another recruit one evening for a visit to town. I approached the Guardroom building and discovered that the Station Police were checking every recruit as he was about to leave via the main gate. I was ordered to face the front and to stand to attention. I was then ordered to turn around and this I did. I was then informed by the Police NCO on duty to return to my billet as my trousers were not properly pressed. Needless to say, I gave up my attempt to leave the Camp. Talking later to other recruits it became patently obvious that the over zealous inspection routine was no more than an official ruse by "the powers that be" to keep new recruits in Camp and out of the town.

Emphasis was there all the time on keeping fit and healthy and the term "FFI" (Free From Infection) was continually being used.

On one particular afternoon we were marched into a hangar in large numbers. We were lined-up in a formation resembling three sides of an elongated oblong and we were told that a Medical Officer would be along shortly to carry out an FFI. It was explained to us that we would be expected to drop our trousers on a given command and display our private parts. The door of the hangar duly opened and in walked a Medical Officer of the Women's Auxiliary Air Force wearing, of course, WAAF uniform. A minor shockwave went through the hangar. The lady was escorted by a male Administration Officer and a senior Staff NCO. The latter called us to attention and followed this with the command, "Drop your slacks! — which we duly did! The atmosphere was almost indescribable as the lady Medical Officer began walking along the ranks peering at recruits' genitals, occasionally assisted by a short stick she was carrying.

By the time she approached our section of the parade, something like ten minutes had elapsed, and in the intervening period the impossible had happened. One recruit standing only a few yards away from me appeared to be sporting an erection. I half expected him to dodge out and disappear but he stood his ground. The Medical Officer passed along the line without a flicker of an expression on her face and when she came to the virile recruit she gave his penis a deft little clout with her stick. The once proud organ withered like the blossom on the vine, only quicker! She then moved smoothly on about her task. The remainder of the Inspection went off without incident. For the rest of his time at Bridgenorth the Airman in mention found himself on the receiving end of a particular kind of unspoken greeting. This took the form of an upward flexing of the right forearm in the direction of the right shoulder!

On the occasion when bad weather prevented outdoor activities, we attended a series of interesting lectures on a range of military topics. One

---

*Author's Note: Service respirators were housed in a khaki canvas container with a separate facemask and filter unit joined together by a corrugated hose, but they did not become standard issue until one had completed one's induction and basic training. We all hated walking about with the cardboard box type of respirator because this told everybody that we were 'Sprogs'. Initially, having a Service respirator had a status value, strange though this may seem.

NB. 'Sprogs' (new recruits) were usually regarded as 'the lowest form of human life'.

of these was on the subject of 'aircraft recognition', which took place in a hut in which were displayed photographs of mainly British and German aircraft. We sat or stood in a group facing a table at which sat the Lecturer, a Flight Sergeant. He gave us a most interesting talk lasting about an hour and he was almost finished when his head and shoulders were suddenly enveloped in a jet of white foam. To say that he was put out is an understatement! I could not believe my eyes. The foam appeared because one of the recruits who had not been able to find a seat for himself had parked his backside on a fire extinguisher, which unfortunately for both parties was operated by a plunger. Purely by chance the nozzle happened to be pointing in the Flight Sergeant's direction. As the recruit sat there with his legs slightly apart, the extinguisher nozzle close to his crotch, it seemed at first as though he was performing a natural function but producing an unnatural result... The offender's reward for this unfortunate incident was to empty the latrine buckets at 6am for the next fourteen days. And there were plenty of them to empty. Thereafter, his nickname was "Foam".

The experience of living in one room with 27 other men was educational in a variety of ways. One recruit, who slept on a nearby bunk, claimed to have already served one year in the Army and did not like it, six months in the Royal Navy and had always been seasick, so he was giving the Air Force a try. I believed his story because he was the only recruit to sport an official Service respirator, the rest of us were tormented with the cardboard-box type of respirator used by the civilian population. None of us squealed on him. He was obviously keen to do military service and having been in all three services must have been some kind of record in 1941.

One other recruit was very fond of his beer and he always seemed to have the money to spend on it. Our weekly pay at that time was still ten shillings so we noticed it when someone else was always in funds. One aspect of his boozing had its unpleasant side because after a night in the pub he managed to wet his bed as often as not. He stayed with us for about a week and was then removed from the hut and probably from the

Royal Air Force. Fortunately for his bunk partner the boozer had been occupying the lower bed. I did not realise that grown-ups did that sort of thing!

Some playing of pranks occurred, particularly on those who had gone off Camp in the evening, the most popular one being that of making the individual a pork-pie bed. This was achieved by re-arranging the blankets so that the bed looked quite normal, but the aperture through which the feet were supposed to enter the bed had been blanked off. The unfortunate recipient would return to the hut after dark (the switching-on of lights was strictly forbidden) and find himself struggling to get into bed. The language at times was quite specific. The following morning the rest of the hut's occupants carried on as though they were surprised to hear about the incident. For the recipient a pork-pie bed was anything but a joke.

On another occasion one bottom bunk occupant, who always slept with his right arm out of the bed and parallel to the floor, came in for a jape that produced an unexpected result.

One of our hut mates produced a hen's egg, uncooked, and gently contrived to feed it into the hand on the outstretched arm of the sleeping Airman. The lights went out, but the expected outburst did not materialise. The jape misfired because the Airman slept through the night and woke up in the morning with an unbroken fresh egg in his hand. This I found quite incredible.

The weeks passed quickly by and I began to feel and behave more and more like a member of a military unit. This in itself I found quite pleasurable. My standard of fitness had improved almost out of recognition and I began to react favourably to the tough discipline to which we were subjected. Our Squad did well at the Passing-Out Parade and our Corporal was a happy man. In my final week I was notified of my posting to an operational flying station at Detling, Kent. This gave me a very warm feeling.

I took away mostly pleasant memories of my weeks at Bridgenorth, but there was one part of my stay I was glad to able to put behind me. A particular Flight Sergeant in our Wing tried on more than one occasion to make me look an idiot in front of the rest of the Flight. He was a man of slight, short build with an austere looking face. I quickly came to the conclusion that he had a complex about tall men – and being six feet four inches tall, I towered over him. The more likely possibility was that he hated policemen.

He was not in attendance on our Squad more than once a week, but when he was he succeeded in putting me through the hoop. He invariably found fault with my shoes and my uniform and if these failed him there was always the haircut. He just could not lose.

He appeared throughout the eight weeks to be seeking the means to get at me. I assumed because he wanted me to do something stupid, he then would be in a position to throw the book at me. When these incidents were taking place, the Squad Corporal kept a discreet distance. I assumed he did this because he did not much care for what the Flight Sergeant was up to.

During one of the Squad drill sessions the Flight Sergeant stood immediately behind me for a number of seconds without moving or saying a word. He then shrieked at the top of his voice "Am I hurting you, Airman". To which I replied "No, Flight Sergeant". Then, at an even shriller pitch he yelled, "Well I bloody well should be because I am standing on your hair!" Within minutes I was in the barber's chair.

On a second occasion we were doing Squad drill with rifles and I dropped a clanger again, much to his delight. It was an early morning parade, the weather was bitterly cold, and in next to no time my hands were frozen. We were at that particular part of the rifle drill movement called "Order Arms" which meant taking the rifle down from the left shoulder, slope position, passing it across the body and returning it in the upright position next to the right foot, butt downwards. I brought the rifle down, but managed to let it slip to the ground in front of my feet. He strolled up to me, then yelled at the top of his voice, "What happened, you sloppy Airman!" I hesitated for a moment, then made the mistake to end all mistakes by replying: "My hands are cold, Flight Sergeant". He fairly leapt in the air with delight. My feeble, ill-advised reply had made his day. I felt a proper twit.

During the last week of the Course I suspect that the Squad got back at him and fortunately he could not pin it on me. We had just gone to bed one night and the lights had been switched off by the hut NCO, when the Flight Sergeant came bounding into the hut and switched the lights on again. He was frothing at the gills because he had just gotten on to his station bicycle when he discovered something was amiss between his legs. Some anonymous person had apparently smeared the saddle with vehicle grease and he assumed it could be one of us, probably me.

I kept my head well down whilst he stormed up and down, threatening the lot of us with all kinds of nasty things if someone didn't own up. No confession of guilt was forthcoming and, having blown his steam, he proceeded to switch off the lights and make for the hut door. He was having difficulty with the Yale lock when one of our number shouted out a rude word which rhymed with crackers. Needless to say, the lights came on again, but most heads were down under the blankets. The deflated Flight Sergeant then left us in peace. I lay in bed almost wetting myself with joy. I doubted if he would do the same.

During my subsequent service as an RAF Policeman at V Region, London, I had occasion to be on duty at a main London Railway Station. My main task on that particular day was to try to apprehend an Airman who had broken out of a camp detention unit and was believed to be making for London via the particular station at which I was on duty.

Lo and behold, who should come through the platform barrier, but my favourite Bridgenorth Flight Sergeant. The expression on his face when he recognised me was ample reward for all that he had put me through during my basic training. I had him just where I wanted me... and he knew it! I took him to our office in the Station concourse and this put the wind up him. I examined his Leave Pass very methodically and I went through the case he was carrying with a fine-toothed comb, in case he was taking home RAF food. As it turned out his Pass and his bag were in order. He was a very relieved Senior NCO when I told him he was free to go. This made me feel quite superior. (N.B. The temptation to name him diminished as I prepared this item for inclusion in the manuscript!)

CHAPTER FOUR

Security at an
Operational Flying Station

RAF Station, Detling, was located on high ground in the neighbourhood of the town of Maidstone, Kent. It was not regarded as one of the frontline operational stations, having only a limited-size, single-track grass runway, but it was an active flying unit, nevertheless. In 1941 it was home to both RAF and Fleet Air Arm Squadrons. The RAF squadrons operated Bristol Blenheim twin-engined bombers and Boulton Paul Defiant single engine night fighters. The Fleet Air Arm Squadrons were operating Fairey Swordfish torpedo bombers and Bristol Beaufort reconnaissance aircraft.

The Blenheims and the Beauforts took part in operations involving shipping and port installations in German occupied France on a regular basis, their success rate was high, but they also had their losses.

Their missions usually commenced at daybreak and lasted about two hours. One particularly hazardous mission against heavy German Warships holed up at Brest, France, stands out in the memory. An Air Gunner from one such mission was severely wounded when his Blenheim was attacked by a German fighter plane. The pilot, a Rhodesian, managed to get the machine back safely, but his fellow Crewman had serious wounds. I mention this one incident because I was present when the plane pancaked on the grass runway and I took part in getting the wounded Airman out of his gun turret. He was still conscious and it was a very distressing business. He was taken to the Unit Medical Centre, he survived the ordeal, but his life as an Airman was finished. The pilot was unhurt and the aircraft was soon back in service.

Strange to relate, one particular early morning raid failed to take place. The crew bus arrived with the flying crews, the planes had been fuelled and armed, but the Armourer, whose job it was to fuse the bombs, had not been woken up in time! The mission and a rendezvous with a fighter escort had to be aborted.

The Station's operational capacity was reduced on more than one occasion when bombs from raiding German aircraft straddled the grass runway, but these raids had more of a nuisance value than anything else. The holes were soon filled-in and operations were quickly resumed.

The Fairey Battle night fighter aircraft were operational most nights when German bombers were operating against London. The techniques and equipment available to night fighter pilots at that time were anything but sophisticated, but the pilots made their presence felt and they had the occasional success. I recall one particularly determined young Flying Officer who could scarcely wait for darkness to come. He became a daily talking point in the messes. He sported the typical handlebar moustache and he was one of the most ebullient extroverts one was ever likely to meet. He was said to have accounted for several German bombers.

On one occasion German fighter bombers carried out a daylight raid on the Station, causing damage to the runway and to a number of key buildings on the site. At the time my thoughts went out, in particular, to an Airman whose job it was to work from a high control tower building. He was in post throughout the raid and he really was a sitting duck. Fortunately for him the German pilots concentrated their efforts on other installations, so he survived. I was well and truly in the open when the first Heinkel bomber dived in and I ran at least two hundred yards to a dugout in a time that would have earned me an Olympic medal! The German planes came in at low level and hedge hopping as they did, they proved hard to hit. They made one bombing or strafing pass and then fled out to sea, flat out at deck level.

The main road to Sittingbourne ran past the main entrance to the Station and the bus stop was only a matter of yards away. At one stage it was noticeable that members of the public waiting for the bus took to using a stack of 500lb bombs which had been off-loaded just outside the station perimeter fence as a seat. The bombs were unarmed, of course, and they were not left there for long. The people concerned probably looked upon them as some kind of novelty and doubtless they told their friends about it when they got home.

Our duties were based on a main Guardroom at the one and only entrance to the Station. We manned the position in shifts, 24 hours a day, and our main task was that of ensuring that only properly authorised individuals and vehicles gained admittance to the Station. We also carried out routine patrols of the total Camp and its perimeter day and night. The Guardroom had its own cellblock and we were responsible for the safekeeping of servicemen who were serving minor sentences for misconduct. The norm was seven days 'jankers', a term used to describe the punishment handed out to those who broke the minor rules. Typical offences were arriving back late from leave, or turning up late for duty. Ground defence of the Station was the responsibility of soldiers from the Royal West Kent Regiment. They provided additional security patrols, but their main task was to provide anti-aircraft cover for the Station. Their main weapon for this purpose was a none-too-effective gun called the Hispano Cannon, but their performance reached very high standards. They dovetailed very well with RAF personnel and they played a valuable role in maintaining tight security arrangements.

The presence of members of the Women's Auxiliary Air Force at Detling was relatively new and it made life both in and out of camp a good deal more pleasant. All-male company day in and day out produced its own problems and a night at the pictures or the local hop with a young lady made a very welcome change. They had a mellowing effect on all of us and they certainly improved the view.

A unit of the Church Army maintained an active presence at the Station and the services they provided made a valuable contribution to the service life both on and off duty. They were one of the less-publicised Service Support Organisations, but they played their part in making our lives more pleasant.

Recreational facilities were limited, but we were able to visit the town of Maidstone during off-duty periods. The bus service was door to door on an hourly basis, and beer, a fairly scarce commodity at that stage of the war, was available at some of the public houses. Needless to say there was a fair amount of competition from Army and Navy personnel stationed in the area and on some occasions this competition got rather vigorous!

As Station Police we were also required to maintain night patrols in the town of Maidstone to deal with rowdiness which occasionally arose among Servicemen when the pubs closed. There was not a lot of this, but when it did take place we had to step in and sort things out.

Occasionally we picked-up a bleeding nose, the odd black eye and the occasional Serviceman who was determined to continue the action. The favourite confrontation seemed to provide for the Army fighting the Royal Air Force, but on occasion the Navy joined in. Most viewed it as good, healthy Inter-Service rivalry, and we handed the offending soldiers and sailors involved over to their respective units. RAF participants were dealt with at the Station Orderly Room the following morning after having spent the night in detention at the Station Guardroom.

The feeling of involvement and the excitement derived from being part of an operational Station, if only for a limited period, proved to be stimulating and satisfying and it was with a measure of disappointment that I was obliged to leave RAF Detling on posting to the RAF Police Training School at Uxbridge, Middlesex.

CHAPTER FIVE

RAF Police School

After a short period of leave at my Shirebrook home, I reported to the Police School at RAF Uxbridge for special training in military police/ security duties. The course was of two months duration, and the curriculum very demanding. Most of our days were spent in the classroom taking instruction in various aspects of Civil Law, Air Force regulations, military law, police/security case work, report writing etc.

Uxbridge was talked about as being the No.1 RAF Depot. Discipline was close to being harsh and we had to pay scrupulous attention to the way we kept our barrack rooms and ourselves. The weekly inspection became almost a nightmare because we were expected to reach absurdly high standards of cleanliness and presentation. The pedantic behaviour of one senior inspecting officer had to be seen to be believed and I doubt if there was an Airman in my Flight who had any respect for him. He was out of this world, but maybe his wife loved him.

Preparing for the weekly parade and barrack room inspection called for a major effort on everyone's part. We worked until we were physically sweating on one occasion, but one small item of blanket fluff behind a cabinet earned us seven days' punishment known as "Fatigues"*.

Getting the uniform precisely pressed, minus bits of cotton, and buttons gleaming, was done with clinical care and precision. Shoes took hours to get up to the preferred standard using the time-honoured spit-and-polish technique. Fortunately, one of our number had been a regular soldier and

---

* "Fatigues" were a mild form of punishment, usually extra duties.

NOBODY'S HERO **41**

THE ROYAL AIR FORCE PROVOST MARSHAL'S BRANCH

In 1829, Sir Robert Peel constituted the first modern civilian Police Force in the United Kingdom. The Royal Air Force Provost Branch is founded on Peel's principles and they still govern its every activity.

The organisation exists for three reasons:
- the Prevention and Detection of Crime
- the Implementation of Security Policy and
- the Maintenance of Discipline.

In all of the above, the Provost Branch has a special responsibility. The authorities place especial trust in the Provost Marshal. He is saddled with a heavy responsibility and the basic training of his Officers and NCOs is designed to teach them how and when to use rank and authority wisely.

The Office of Provost Marshal

The office of Provost Marshal dates back to at least the 16th century. Articles of War promulgated by Charles I in 1629 empowered the Marshal's Court' to "hear, judge and determine any act done by the soldiers". The "Provost General's" duties were summarized in the concluding article of the code: "The Provost must have a horse allowed him, and some soldiers to attend him, and all the rest commanded to obey him and assist him, or else the Service will suffer, for he is but one man and must correct many and therefore he cannot be beloved. And he must be riding from one garrison to another, to see that the soldiers do not outrage nor scathe about the country"

In 1642 there was a broadening of the Provost Marshal's responsibilities to include protection of the soldiery and what we would now call counter-intelligence. At that time, the Earl of Essex, Commander of the Parliamentary Army, published his *Lawes and Ordinances of Warre* which became the foundation of all subsequent articles of war.

Here it was decreed that the Provost Marshal and his underlings would "look to the proportions of the true weights and measures of merchants selling victuals in camps". Of far more importance was the responsibility laid on the Provost Marshal for counter-intelligence. For the first time it was formally recognised that police work and security in the Service could not be separated and it became the Provost Marshal's duty to:

> *"discover the lurking subtleties of spies, and by learning the true interpretation of men's words, looks, manners, forms and habits of apparel, to be able to turn the insides of their heart outwards, and to pull out that devil of malicious deceit, though he lie and in never so dark a corner, and truly a better service cannot be done, nor is there any art sooner learnt if a man will apply his knowledge but seriously thereto".*

Later ordinances changed the role and powers of the Provost Marshal. His duties included those of executioner and the holding of prisoners in custody. By general order of the Duke of Wellington in 1811, the Provost Marshal was made responsible for the custody of prisoners and the preservation of good order and discipline among the armed forces. He was empowered also to punish summarily those committing a breach of discipline in his view. His assistants, who were not commissioned officers, could exercise summary powers of punishment when it was necessary to make an example of an offender for a particular crime. They had no powers to inflict capital punishment.

In 1829, the Articles of War expressly provided for the appointment and powers of the Provost Marshal, and in 1879 his powers of punishment were curtailed by an Act of Parliament. The powers of his office are currently described in the Army and Air Force Acts, Section 74.

Transfer of police responsibilities from the Army to the RAF

Following the constitution of the Royal Air Force in 1918, responsibility for the policing of stations and units was soon transferred from the Army to the Royal Air Force and was completed in 1919. During the transition period, liaison was maintained between Military Assistant Provost Marshals and District Discipline Officers appointed by the Royal Air Force to deal with matters affecting discipline.

what he did not know about getting oneself ready for a parade and inspection was probably not worth knowing. It was a common event for us to sit around whilst he demonstrated the art of pressing trousers so that the crease was like the edge of a sharp knife. His skills with buttons and the webbing belt we had to wear were a great help, but the total input in man-hours still had to be faced by each of us individually. Some nights we were known to start at 5:30pm and finish just in time for lights out at 10pm. The term used to describe this activity was "bull".

Probably the biggest pantomime of all at RAF Uxbridge was getting the barrack room itself ready for the weekly inspection. The floor was covered with battleship linoleum and this had to shine till it resembled a mirror. Beds had to be placed so that when viewed from one end they were not a centimetre out of line. Blankets had to be folded in the same, precise way on every bed. Lockers and their contents had to be thoroughly checked, one hair on a comb or brush was a disaster and the Airman responsible was disciplined. Once the floor had been polished, movement around the floor was achieved in our socks or sliding along, ski fashion, on the rags we had used as part of the polishing operation. Heaven protect the Airman who did it otherwise.

Demanding drill sessions on the Square were succeeded by a weekly Commanding Officer's parade, which the Jews and the Roman Catholics, by choice could miss. Once the parade had assembled, the cry went out "fall out the Roman Catholics and the Jews", and off they went.

Ad hoc oral and written examinations were a feature of the course and those who failed to achieve a certain standard were gradually excluded and posted to other duties. The survival rate was probably four in five, so our numbers gradually dwindled.

The heavy demands made on us on most days were eased at intervals by athletic activities, the facilities for which were first-class. The Station was very well equipped and most outdoor and indoor pursuits were available. The food was first-class and plentiful and together with regular bouts of physical training we began to feel a good deal fitter than we were when we began the course. The training staff, as often as not, were men who had achieved national or international fame in one or other branch of sport or recreation, and it was a joy to be in their company.

During the two months I was stationed at Uxbridge I did not leave the confines of the Station on one single occasion. I was a single man and I saw no reason to do so. I played soccer regularly and had some success at athletic meetings. The Station's first eleven soccer team was made up almost entirely of top name professionals from the Football League. Several of them were well known at International level. I managed to make the second eleven which was made up mainly of players from the lower Divisions of the League.

The final week of the Course was devoted to tests and examinations and I was pleased to achieve an above average pass mark. My time as a civilian Police Constable had helped me considerably. I was made a NCO (Non-Commissioned Officer) with the rank of Corporal. I had only been in the Service for about five months, so I had made reasonable progress. Most of my basic requirements were taken care of by the Service, but there was disappointment that our weekly pay parade seldom yielded more than ten shillings. Service pay continued to be shrouded in mystery and asking questions seldom produced satisfactory answers.

The Course having been completed, I was posted from Uxbridge to RAF Police Headquarters, located in a large Country house at Burnham Beeches, Buckinghamshire.

Author's Notes

i) During the time I was at RAF Uxbridge the Station also housed a Medical Unit to which members of air crews were referred when experiencing special medical problems. John Hannah, the RAF's fourth holder of the Victoria Cross in the war, was one such person. On some days he was to be seen passing time sitting on top of a surface air raid shelter, looking totally dejected. It was impossible to describe one's feelings at seeing one of the war's heroes aimlessly whiling away the days.

(ii) In the NAAFI canteen one day, I became acquainted with a young man who wore a pilot's brevet on his blouse, but who had no rank at all other than "Airman". He had flown operationally and whilst diving a plane had damaged his ears. As a member of the aircrew he had been entitled to wear a Sergeant's stripes, but when he was downgraded medically, the rank of Sergeant was taken away. He was "on detachment" at Uxbridge awaiting a medical board. He was hoping that the outcome would be that he would be allowed to continue his RAF Service in some other capacity. I found all this hard to comprehend.

CHAPTER SIX

Top Secrets and Tragedies

After undertaking a short spell of basic police/security tasks at RAF Burnham, special teams of NCOs were formed principally for the purpose of providing security cover for top secret security projects associated with prototype aircraft being developed (for the RAF) by privately owned aircraft manufacturers. I became a member of one of these teams.

Probably the most important of these projects was concerned with two planes that were to be powered for the first time by jet engines. The first of these was a prototype aircraft known as the Gloster Whittle E28/39. The body was built by the Gloster Aircraft Company at Hucclecote, Gloucestershire and the engine by Power Jets Limited at Lutterworth, Leicestershire. The brains behind the jet engine was Frank Whittle, who was later knighted for his achievements.

We assumed responsibility for the machine's overall security during one of its prototype development phases which took place at the RAF Station, Shennington, near Banbury, Oxon.

When we arrived, the partly built machine was already housed in a hangar specially built on one of the Station's extremities. The Security classification being 'TOP SECRET', round the clock physical surveillance was necessary. (Shennington was a satellite of a main bomber base at Moreton in the Marsh, Glos). We were billeted in a hut on an aircraft dispersal site about a mile away from the Station HQ buildings. The only other "occupants" of the site were three Wellington bombers that took part, whilst we were there, in the RAF's first 'thousand bomber raid' on Germany. They all returned safely after an eight-hour operation. Their

The Gloster/Whittle E28/39 prototype jet aircraft outside a hangar at RAF Shennington.

main role was as training aircraft for newly recruited aircrews. They were in the air day and night taking part in training activities known as "circuits and bumps". They took off, made a fifteen to twenty minute circuit, landed and took off again... hence the description.

The prototype aircraft was a single-seat fighter, but there was something different about it. The nose and tail sections were shrouded for the first few days and this added to the mystery. There was no propeller or engine visible and when the wraps were taken off, there appeared to be a hole back and front about the same circumference as a dustbin. Technology being what it was up to that time, we found it hard to comprehend that the machine was not going to be fitted with a propeller.

After four weeks or so we were told that the machine was to be taken out on to the concrete apron at the front of the hangar so that the "engine could be fired". The Gloster Aircraft Company test pilot, Gerry Sayer, arrived and the firing operation commenced. This proved to be quite

---

AUTHOR'S NOTE: Frank Whittle obtained an Admiralty patent on his jet engine prior to the War, but Britain did not develop the potential of this invention until hostilities ended.

NOBODY'S HERO

sensational particularly when a sizeable jet of flame shot out of the tail end aperture of the aircraft. It was an incredible sight, but as the Engineers remained perfectly calm, we soon came to realise that this was all according to plan. The engine was run for about fifteen minutes and the verdict was that a satisfactory test had taken place.

An interesting element in the secrecy surrounding the aircraft was that during the period whilst the pre-flight build operations were being finalised in the hangar the word "jet" was never once used. I, personally, had no idea what the new propulsion technique was about, and until the firing operation took place I remained convinced that one day an engine with a propeller would arrive and be installed.

The next stage was the carrying out of taxiing trials to test the undercarriage and other control mechanisms. These took place some days later with Gerry Sayer at the controls. One of the tarmac runways at the Station was used for this purpose and one of our number was required to ride a hotted-up Norton motor cycle behind the aircraft with instructions to help get the pilot out if things went wrong.

We rarely visited the station proper and we were forbidden leave of absence whilst the project remained on site at Shennington. This was a security measure.

The physical duty of guarding the hangar was in the hands of a team of young Army OTC (Officers' Training Corps) cadets* from various Public Schools. Technically, they were under our control whilst on site. They were twelve in number and their services had been procured by arrangement with the Gloster Aircraft Company. They were proficient young soldiers; they all carried the Short Magazine Lee Enfield rifle and they certainly knew how to use it. They were dressed as private soldiers in khaki uniforms, puttees and ammunition boots. Their headdress was a beret. They physically manned the area of the hangar 24 hours a day and

---

*Author's Note: One was the son of Norman Wilkinson, the celebrated (naval) artist. Another, I shall always have cause to remember, was a young man named Selby-Lowndes who I believe was later to lose his life as a bomber pilot during a night mission over Germany. His name came back to me in 1982 when my wife and I were preparing the manuscript for Wing Commander Michael Renaut's story of the Halifax bomber, "Terror by Night" (published by Kimber & Co in 1982).

during the whole of our time at Shennington there was not one single incident where their security arrangement was penetrated. They came from good class families, performed their duties admirably and were easily managed. They were billeted in a hut next to ours on the aircraft dispersal site and they responded to RAF discipline and requirements in an exemplary manner.

Nothing really untoward happened during the taxiing trials and the machine was eventually cleared for test flying. Several flights then took place at intervals and on one occasion an Air Rank Officer (the equivalent of an Admiral in the Navy or a General in the Army) representing the Ministry of Aircraft Production (MAP) arrived on an inspection visit.

The E28/39 was wheeled out on to the apron and the engine was fired. The Air Marshal had with him a walking stick with an amber handle. Somewhat to everyone's surprise, he pushed the walking stick in the direction of the exhaust flame and ended up with only the amber handle and about eighteen inches of walking stick left in his hand. He had the presence of mind to roar with laughter, but I wonder if the result was quite what he expected? The remainder of his visit was taken up with a most satisfactory test flight, with Gerry Sayer at the controls.

Shortly afterwards, the Shennington part of the programme for the E28/39 was pronounced complete, the machine was loaded on to a "Queen Mary" road transporter and taken back to the Gloster Aircraft works at Hucclecote. We returned to HQ at Burnham not appreciating the fact that we had been parties, in a minor way, to the making of aviation history. We were later delighted to hear it being said that the introduction of the E28/39 into the world of aviation was one of the best kept secrets of the war.

Gerry Sayer's first day arrival at RAF Shennington was interesting because he marked the occasion with an aerobatic display in his beloved Gloster Gladiator biplane. He could make that machine do anything. I believe it now stands at the Shuttleworth Aircraft Museum.Gerry Sayer was

The Martin-Baker MB3 aircraft.

recognised as an outstanding test pilot. Sadly, he was to lose his life in a test flying accident.

The second secret prototype aircraft project was concerned with a single-seater, single-engined fighter being produced by the Martin Baker Aircraft Company of Higher Denham, Buckinghamshire. The machine was designated the MB3 and it was powered by the H-type Napier Sabre engine generating 2,000 horsepower. This was a piston engine driving a three bladed propeller.

We were posted-in to the RAF station at Wing, Buckinghamshire, an Officers' Training Unit within 92 Group Bomber Command. The aircraft arrived the following day. It was housed in a separate hangar and we again

Author's Note: A lady named Amy Johnson, who in the 1920s became world famous for being the first woman Aviator to fly solo from England to Australia, was taught to fly by Captain Baker. Amy was killed in 1941 when she was ferrying a wartime aircraft for service with the Royal Air Force. There were no navigational aids such as radio or radar in those days and flights were planned on maps using the technique know as "dead reckoning". Amy ran into appalling weather conditions, got lost, ran out of fuel, baled out over water and was drowned.

EJECTOR SEATS

It is in the design and production of ejection seats that the name Martin-Baker has become best known. In this field, the company has created an international reputation and established itself as the market leader. For his personal work on ejection seat design, Sir James Martin (pictured here) is recognised internationally as a pioneer and expert and throughout the world many tributes have been paid to his work. In June 1950 he was appointed an Officer of the Order of the British Empire, being promoted to Commander in the Order in 1957. In 1951 he was elected Fellow of the Royal Aeronautical Society and awarded its Wakefield Gold Medal in 1952 for work on ejection seats. The Royal Aero Club of the United Kingdom in 1964 awarded him its Gold Medal, and in 1965 he was created a Knight Batchelor.

In the sphere of air safety, the United States of America has honoured Sir James in an exceptional way by the award in 1958 of the Laura Taber-Barbour Air Safety Award, given for outstanding contribution to air safety. The award, which is within the jurisdiction of the Flight Safety Foundation Incorporated of the United States of America, was on this occasion given for the first time to a non-American.

A vast amount of basic research work has been done by the company, not only in the mechanics and chemistry of ejection seat design, but also in the extremely important physiological area, a science about which, in the early days, information was notably scanty. The results obtained have been translated into an operationally efficient ejection seat, fully automatic, capable of saving life by getting air crews away from the aircraft in dire distress under extremely difficult circumstances, in which escape would otherwise be improbable. Martin-Baker seats are fitted in jet aircraft of the Royal Air Force, Royal Navy, US Navy and US Air Force, French, German and Italian Air Forces as well as the aircraft of many other air forces.

carried out round the clock surveillance duties. This was a machine with which Mr James Martin(later Sir James Martin, the inventor of the aircraft ejector seat) and Captain Valentine Baker were intimately involved. Mr Martin, an Engineer, had overall responsibility for the aircraft as a machine and Captain Baker was the test pilot.

Work went on for some days to prepare and ground test the machine for flight and on a given day the first flight took place, successfully. The performance of the aircraft was expected to be equal to that of the best single-seater fighters in service with the RAF at that time. One particular flight quite early in the programme, proved to be quite spectacular, and there was considerable excitement in the hangar when Captain Baker taxied in. Among ourselves we christened the machine "The Thunderbolt".

Captain Baker's wife usually attended on the days when the machine was flying and she proved to be a most intrepid lady, making the journey from their home to Wing on an autocycle. Someone said it was at least a thirty mile journey each way.

Development work continued to be carried out on the aircraft, everyone seemed to be pleased with the way the programme was going, but events then took a fateful turn for the worse. Further flights were programmed, but on one never-to-be-forgotten day, 12th September 1942, the Sabre engine on the MB3 failed shortly after take-off and the machine crashed on a neighbouring farm. Captain Baker, in an attempt to save the aircraft whilst executing a difficult forced landing, crash landed the plane in a field and was killed. The engine separated from the fuselage and ended up some yards away. The fuselage fractured but, before it went up in flames, and at considerable risk to himself, Mr Alf Woolhead, a farmhand who was 'sweeping-up' after haymaking in the next field, managed to get Captain Baker out of the cockpit and laid his body on the ground. There were no signs of life. Mr Woolhead later observed Mr James Martin sitting sobbing in a nearby ditch. The RAF Medical service collected Captain Baker's body and removed it to the Station mortuary. The following day the RAF collected the remains of the MB3 aircraft.

The shock for all concerned was tremendous. The tragedy brought the project to an abrupt end and we returned to our Burnham Headquarters, feeling thoroughly dejected and demoralised.

Captain Baker, like Gerry Sayer, was a master pilot and he frequently treated the personnel at RAF Station Wing to aerobatic displays in a Tiger Moth aeroplane. His piece-de-resistance was a "falling leaf" finish, which ended up with him gliding the Tiger smoothly on to the apron in front of the Martin Baker hangar almost as though he was parking his car. On one occasion, as he climbed out of the cockpit, a group of RAF Aircrew types applauded. The Captain seemed delighted at this.

Some forty years later I was playing golf in a foursome at Leighton Buzzard Golf Club and a discussion about the wartime airfield at RAF Wing took place. A certain Mr Bunny Winter, who at that time farmed the land where the Martin Baker plane had crashed, was able to tell us that he saw the plane come down and was one of the first members of the public at the scene; a truly interesting coincidence after a 40-year interval.

It was later stated that James Martin never forgot the fearless, skilful and resolute pilot, and many considered that it may have been this painful tragedy that really fired him to develop aircraft ejector seats which are today in use by the Air Forces all over the world.

The third secret prototype aircraft was a twin-engined jet also produced by the Gloster Aircraft Company. This machine turned out to be the forerunner of the Gloster Meteor, the first British Jet fighter aircraft to enter into RAF squadron service.

The location for our security operations with the Meteor was the RAF Station at Newmarket, which for the duration of the war embraced practically the whole of the famous Racecourse acreage and buildings.

We were billeted separately from the rest of the Station personnel in a Nissen hut. The aircraft arrived from Hucclecote and was installed in a secluded hangar adjacent to the famous Rowley Mile racetrack. On this occasion we were again made responsible for the total security of the

---

Author's Note: The Ras Prince Monolulu was well known at race meetings all over the United Kingdom. On race days he wore the most colourful, flowing tribal robes and on his head he sported a crown embellished with feathers. His famous cry "I gotta horse!" was familiar to millions.

NOBODY'S HERO

Henry Valentine Baker with star pupil Amy Johnson.

Cpt. Henry Valentine Baker MC DFC RFC

aircraft in its hangar and during its trial runs. The precise location was relatively remote and therefore fairly ideal for hush-hush activities. Unlike its predecessor, the Gloster Whittle E28/39, this particular aircraft had never been off the ground.

Horse racing activity was continuing on a part of the course, but on a very limited scale. The classic race, the St Leger, was run whilst we were there and proved to be one of the highlights of our off-duty time at Newmarket. Weeks in advance of the race a local farrier gave us a hot tip, a horse named 'Herringbone'. Race day arrived and we made our way to the track. We foolishly ignored the farrier's advice and backed another runner tipped by that colourful racing tipster, The Ras Prince Monolulu.*

Herringbone won the race at long odds. The horse tipped by The Ras Prince finished tenth. We provided him with board accommodation — on the QT of course — for the days of the St Leger meeting. The St Leger is normally run at Doncaster, but during the war years the venue was switched to Newmarket.

For Armed Forces personnel on low pay, the only effective way to get around when off duty was by hitchhiking. During the war, petrol was severely rationed and traffic at the best of times was light, but there was scarcely a vehicle that did not respond to the traditional thumb-up signalling routine used by Service hitchhikers.

Hitchhiking was also not without its challenges and I ran headlong into one of these when one evening I decided to hitch hike from RAF Newmarket to the town of Huntingdon with the intention of seeing a film at the local cinema.

The main road I needed to take was close to the Station entrance and I had no sooner got there when a large, black Wolseley limousine responded to my hitchhike signal. As it drew up I could not help but notice a sticker on the windscreen bearing the letters 'AM' (Air Ministry). I thanked the driver for stopping and climbed in to the front alongside him.

I knew immediately that I was in the presence of somebody important. We began to talk and after a while he asked me what kind of work I was doing in the RAF. I replied to the effect that I was in Motor Transport, a downright lie, of course, but I had adopted this tactic on previous lifts because I did not want to get drawn into a conversation about the secret aircraft we were looking after.

After another twenty minutes of motoring, the driver stopped the car, went into a GPO telephone kiosk and made a call. When he came back, the car would not start and I immediately began to feel distinctly uncomfortable. Having told him that I was in Motor Transport, when I was not, I realised that I was very near to being caught out. He quietly cursed the car and the engine, which still refused to start. He then turned to me and commented that perhaps it was lucky that he had picked me up, being a Transport man.

I had no choice but to do something that looked convincing, so I climbed out and released the car bonnet. Having been around motorbikes, jeeps and lorries for some time, I was not entirely ignorant of the rudiments of an internal combustion engine, but this was a huge looking engine such as I had never seen before, so I wasn't exactly brimming with confidence.

I finally discovered that the shaft running through the starter motor was stuck, so using one of his tool kit spanners I gave it some attention. Suddenly, it freed itself and when I called out for him to try again the engine sprang to life.

We completed the journey, but by this time I decided I had had enough excitement to satisfy my requirements for one evening. I was too late for the cinema, anyway. I crossed to the opposite side of the road and was lucky enough to hitch a return lift to the Camp gates without further problems. When hitchhiking after that, I took to telling people that I worked as an Administrator in Station Headquarters.

Whilst at Newmarket I was permitted a long week-end leave pass and I used the opportunity to pay a visit to my home near Nottingham. Hitch hiking this time paid off because a lorry belonging to Boots the Chemists passed the main gates of RAF Newmarket and the driver responded to my hitchhike signal. This provided me with transport all the way to Nottingham, which was nine tenths of my journey home. I was able to reimburse the lorry driver and his mate by giving them the farrier's tip for the St Leger Classic, 'Herringbone'. They were both betting men and when Herringbone won the Leger at long odds they collected handsomely from the Bookmaker, having put a substantial joint sum of money on the horse. They said that from their one bet they had each won more than a whole week's wages!

One of our periodic cross-countrys to and from our Burnham HQ to Newmarket produced an especially interesting development. We were eight men in a Fordson 15cwt truck and travelling as we were on a stretch of open road we came across a motorist whose Jaguar motor car was halfway into a roadside ditch. We stopped, offered help, and this was warmly accepted.

The driver, a well-dressed civilian, was obviously a VIP. He made a point of chatting to us as we worked on his car and he mentioned that he was an airman himself. We exchanged the usual glances at each other when he made this remark because it seemed to be the case that whenever RAF people were in pubs or railway carriages there was always a man present who had served in the Flying Corps in the 1914-18 War. This was another such occasion, we assumed.

Getting the car back on to the road was a bigger task than we had bargained for, but by using a towrope and a fair amount of muscle we eventually succeeded. We then noticed that a front tyre was flat, so we replaced the wheel with the spare from the boot. The jacking system on the car was unserviceable so getting the body up sufficiently high to make the wheel swap was really demanding. There was a lot of solid metal in a pre-war Jaguar motor car.

---

*Author's Note: Sir Alan Cobham (1894-1973) was an Aviation legend in his own lifetime. His name and his aviation achievements in the 1920s and 30s were applauded and talked about across the world. In 1923 he won the Britannia Trophy for being the first British pilot to cross the English Channel in an ultra-light plane. He won the prestigious King's Cup Air Race in 1924. He flew London-Capetown in 1925/6. He flew London-Australia in 1926. He was a Founder Member of the Guild of Airline Pilots and Navigators. Millions saw the Cobham Flying Circus as it toured the United Kingdom. He was truly one of the greatest aviators of all time.

The prototype Gloster Meteor on the Rowley Mile racecourse at RAF Newmarket.

The whole job took the best part of an hour, our uniforms and our hands were in a bit of a state, but I think we were all satisfied that we had done the right thing. I climbed back into the cab of our truck alongside the driver. The car driver then came across, thanked us profusely and handed my colleague a £1 note which he said he hoped we would use to 'buy us all a drink' (£1 in those days would buy twenty pints of beer, so we felt well rewarded). With that he took his place behind the wheel of his care and drove off. We were about to drive off ourselves when my driver colleague noticed that beneath the pound note was a visiting card. Printed on the card were the words, 'Sir Alan Cobham'.★

The physical training instructor at RAF Newmarket at that time was Eric (Boy) Boon, the British, European and Empire boxing champion.

Eric came from nearby Chatteris and part of his gymnasium equipment had been installed in Jockey Club premises, which for the duration of the war became part of the RAF Station.

Having had some boyhood training, I went along to the gymnasium and took part in training/sparring sessions with other Airmen. This led to me being included in the Station boxing team, which regularly took part in programmes staged at other RAF Stations and the Universities of

Oxford and Cambridge. These programmes were usually staged on Friday nights in village halls and they were well attended by the general public. A modest charge for admission was made and the proceeds usually went to the 'Battle of Britain Fund' or 'War Weapons Week'. RAF Newmarket were able to put out a team at all the standard amateur boxing weights, except heavyweight. Being six feet four and fourteen and a half stones, I was persuaded to fill this gap and, as a result, most of my Friday nights were fully occupied for some weeks to come. The Station ran a 40-seat bus to the matches and so it was usually full with RAF and WAAF personnel from the Station, supporting their Team.

I had a run of successes and I enjoyed taking part, but after a few weeks, the build-up of bruises, sore ribs, loose teeth and black eyes began to take the shine off the activity. At one stage I took part in three contests in four weeks, which was a bit much!

The social events following the fights, usually held at a local pub, were good fun and we were seldom short of food, drink and merrymaking. A feature of the return journeys to camp was the singing of the usual bawdy songs – which the WAAFs seemed to enjoy as much as we did!

One outstanding night at Cambridge featured one of the top dance bands of the day, Nat Gonella and his Georgians. Nat himself led the Band and they put on a really entertaining show. I had won my bout so I was feeling pretty good.

I eventually sustained a nose injury during a fight which put paid to my participation as a member of the Station boxing team. I was due to have a re-match contest at RAF Mildenhall with a Scotsman whom I had beaten previously. I changed at the Hall and there was a long wait for me because the Heavyweight contest was always the last on the bill. I was sitting in the dressing room when someone came in and informed me that my intended opponent was unwell and would not be taking part.

I was in the process of getting dressed again and becoming a spectator, when someone came into the changing room and told me that there was

---

* After the war I had the pleasure of meeting Bill Thorburn again at one of London's top Theatres where he was playing one of the leading roles in the hit musical *Oklahoma*.

a local member of the Home Guard who was willing to fight me. I agreed to this subject to the understanding that he, like me, was a novice.

An hour or so later the Home Guard man and I were mixing it in the ring for three furious three minute rounds of boxing. There was blood all over the place. The contest was declared a draw, but my face was a hell of a mess. I had a cut under one eye, I knew my nose had been broken, my mouth was pretty sore, I had black eyes and I was spitting blood. I later discovered that the Home Guard "novice" had been an Army boxing champion for years with about fifty good class fights under his belt!

The evening ended with the usual party at a pub and at one stage I recall drinking from a pint beer mug that had a foreign body in it. The foreign body turned out to be one of my teeth!

I had little sleep that night and early the next morning I went to see the Medical Officer about my injuries. I was whipped in to the RAF Hospital at Ely where the surgeon removed a blood clot and repaired my broken nose, etc. The surgeon said I had had a close shave. I believe the medical term was *Haematoma*. He entered on my RAF medical record that I was forbidden to take any further part in boxing. I enjoyed a week's sick leave at my home. The dent in my nose has been with me ever since.

Work on the Meteor aircraft and ground trial runs was carried out over a period of weeks. A feature of the ground trial runs was the extensive damage done to the sacred Rowley Mile race track turf by the heat from the plane's engines. Much to our disappointment, the aircraft did not take to the air because the heat from the two engines was affecting the tailplane and its control mechanisms. This automatically brought the trials to an end and the aircraft was taken back to the works at Hucclecote. The next time I saw a Meteor Aircraft, it was in service with a Royal Air Force Squadron, with a modified tail configuration.

Following cessation of the Newmarket project, we returned to the house at Burnham. Some leave was taken and life there was fairly relaxed. The main recreational activity was centred on the Unit soccer team, which was made up of League professionals and a nucleus of good amateurs. We played at least one game a week and capped an interesting season by winning the Maidenhead Hospital Cup. We were presented with handsome silver and gold medals.

A rather special feature of our sporting activity at Burnham was our lady soccer team Trainer. She was the WAAF Medical Orderly at Burnham. Her name was Rita and we all thought she was just plain gorgeous — which she was! She was also a first-class football team trainer. The in-joke at the time was that we looked forward to being injured, so that she could come and tend to us.

An unusual feature of the house was the presence of peacocks and peahens in the grounds. They moved around at will and it was quite a common experience for one of them to flop out of the trees, after dark, and land on your shoulder. The first time it happened to me I nearly had a fit. The peahens were the offenders, not the peacocks.

An occasional VIP visitor to the mess was Amy Johnson's husband, Jim Morrison. At the time, Jim was flying ferry missions across the Atlantic bringing much needed bomber additions to RAF Squadrons. Jim's operating base at the time was White Waltham, near Maidenhead, a unit forming part of the total aircraft ferry activity. Jim, like Amy, was a world famous aviator in his own right, and he and Amy made epic flights together to different parts of the World. They were both aviation celebrities in their own lifetimes.

Evening leisure was as often as not taken at a Bracknell pub where beer was usually available. One of our number was a Scot named William Thorburn* who had a fine tenor voice. Bill entertained us from his extensive repertoire and one evening turned out to be rather special. Bill usually got on his feet around 8.30pm, and on this particular evening there was a distinguished-looking gentleman having a drink in the bar. After listening to one of Bill's numbers he said he was going to see if he could persuade a pianist he knew to join us. At about 9pm the gentleman reappeared with a distinguished-looking lady who proceeded to accompany

Bill on the piano. For the next hour and a half we were treated to a never-to-be-forgotten musical concert. The gentleman insisted on paying for the drinks and Bill and the lady pianist entertained us quite regally. We did not have the nerve to ask who the lady was, but someone suggested it was Moura Lympany, the celebrated Concert pianist. Someone else said he was certain it was the equally distinguished and celebrated pianist Eileen Joyce. We never did find out.

A journey I made from Burnham one day on a motorcycle for the purpose of visiting an American Air Base turned out to be a truly traumatic occasion. As I approached the Station, aircraft, mainly Flying Fortress bombers, were taking off at fairly frequent intervals.

At the point where their flight paths crossed the road on which I was travelling, these aircraft had achieved a height of a few hundred feet. To my total horror and shock one of the Flying Fortresses exploded immediately above my head and a body came hurtling down to earth and landed in a field about four hundred yards from the road I was travelling on.

I had ceased to pay attention to what I was doing and before I knew where I was, I was under the motorbike in a ditch. I was none the worse for the spill, so I made my way across the field as best I could. The field had been ploughed and the ground was very wet, and sticky. I was up to the ankles in heavy soil. I eventually reached the Airman who was dressed in an American flying suit and helmet. He had been thrown out of the aircraft and had landed feet first in an almost upright position. His legs were buried almost up to the knees and his body was fairly upright. He appeared to be dead and when I touched his face and hands, there was no sign of life. I had no means of digging him out and I was afraid to do anything that I felt might make his injuries worse, in case he was still alive, but unconscious. Momentarily I was stuck to know what to do for the best.

I imagined the Airman to be in his middle twenties. This was without doubt one of the worst moments of my life and I was tremendously relieved when an American Air Force ambulance arrived with a Doctor and a recovery team. The Doctor pronounced the Airman dead. I abandoned my intended visit to the Station and rode back to Burnham almost in a trance.

A few days after this incident I was transferred to the Headquarters of the Provost Marshal for the London area. Its precise designation was 'PM Branch, 5 Region'. The address, Exhibition Road, South Kensington.

CHAPTER SEVEN

Security Duties in the Capital

Five Region was the London and District Headquarters of the Provost Marshal's branch of the Royal Air Force. Its area of responsibility was the whole of London and some of its surrounding urban areas. Control of the Branch was vested in Officers designated as Deputy and/or Assistant Provost Marshals. Non-Commissioned Officers (NCOs) of both sexes were the main operational arm of the Branch carrying out a range of police and security functions.

The main day-to-day duties performed were:

(i)   the security of Air Ministry properties and establishments in London;

(ii)   the investigation of crime at R A F establishments;

(iii)   the detection and apprehension of 'deserters and masqueraders';

(iv)   checking that RAF personnel using the main railway termini were properly documented and authorised to be using public transport

(v)   acting as a source of general information for members of the RAF in transit to and from London

Duties were mainly carried out in uniform, but some plain-clothes activities were also undertaken where concealed identity assisted operations.

Many men and women whose homes were in London had enlisted in the Royal Air Force and this meant that they were in transit to and from

London in substantial numbers most days of the week. This created the demand for PM Branch NCOs to be on duty at the main railway termini to assist and help control those in transit.

The West End of London remained a major entertainment centre during the war and it attracted large numbers of servicemen and women on leave. These circumstances combined to create an incessantly high level of demand for PM Branch NCOs to be on duty in Central London itself.

Absentees and deserters thought to be in the Region usually had homes or relatives living in London and on occasion families were known to go to extraordinary lengths to conceal them. In these cases, painstaking enquiries and observations were called for, but the apprehension rate was high.

One particularly intriguing case of concealment took us several months to resolve. The Airman in question lived in Southeast London and several surprise visits to his home failed to find him. Neighbours kept making the point to us that the man being sought was present in the house when Branch representatives called. Finally, a search warrant, backed by the Metropolitan Police, brought the house under closer internal scrutiny, including the lifting of floor coverings.

Under a carpet in one room a small cubicle built under the floorboards was discovered and, there, lying quietly on a mattress was the reluctant Airman. He later confessed to having been hiding in the cubicle on the occasion of two previous visits by Branch representatives.

'Masquerading' was also an occasional feature of wartime life in the Armed Forces. This manifested itself in a variety of forms but it all added up to the individuals posing as something they were not. For example an airman might award himself three stripes (rank of sergeant) and a pilot's wings. This particular kind of masquerade seldom succeeded because the offenders were easily detectable. There was usually something about their deportment and manner that gave them away, but doubtless some of them went undetected. On one occasion a male and a female masquerader were strolling arm in arm in Piccadilly Circus, the male dressed as a Flight Lieutenant, the female dressed as a WAAF Pilot Officer. They were picked up within hours of arriving for a weekend in Town, mainly because they did not look convincing; as it turned out neither of them held commissions in the Service.

One particularly amusing masquerade was uncovered when I was working in plain clothes on special duties. My job was to make observations on a block of flats used by foreign embassy personnel. Whilst standing across the street from the Embassy, an airman, who from all appearances was new to the service, walked past me and disappeared down the steps of a nearby public convenience. Half an hour later, the same airman reappeared in the street but by this time he had promoted himself to Sergeant. His brand new stripes had scarcely seen the light of day when he was checked and arrested. In his pocket were needles and a partly-used bobbin of cotton. He must have thought his luck was really out. I had one hell of a job keeping a straight face.

The arrest of another masquerader resulted in a colleague severely damaging a shoulder. We were walking down a footpath leading to New Scotland Yard when we noticed two policemen escorting a man wearing Army uniform. Suddenly the prisoner broke clear of his escort and came charging towards us. My colleague brought him down with a rugby tackle, damaging his shoulder in the process. We pinned the man down until his escort caught up with him. Apparently, he was a private soldier who had been masquerading as a Sergeant Major! My colleague suffered from the after-effects of his intervention for some weeks.

The presence in the RAF of people with unusual sexual propensities manifested themselves among both sexes and occasionally called for PM Branch action. Service life, as often as not, was undertaken in barrack room conditions and homosexuality and lesbianism were not tolerated, and had to be dealt with, usually by discharging the deviants from the service.

With an intake running into thousands a month, it was inevitable that some of the recruits inducted were a bit 'unusual' and one of the peculiarities that stuck in my mind was the discovery that under his RAF uniform, one detainee was found to be wearing 'jazzy' women's underwear. He had been observed soliciting in a public convenience and brought to V Region HQ by one of our West End patrol teams. Detainees in this category were invariably asked to take a bath; the game for them was then over.

Occasionally, politically subversive members of the Service came to notice and were dealt with quickly and effectively. Peace campaigners in military units were also a problem calling for swift action.

The Branch was occasionally required to provide guards of honour for special occasions, sometimes involving members of the Royal Family. I took part in one of these on an occasion when the Duke of Kent had been invited to open a club for Service personnel in Central London. My two guard-of-honour companions for this function were the celebrated Surrey and England test cricketers, Eric and Alec Bedser. We formed a three-man contingent. The opening ceremony was due to be broadcast by the BBC at lunchtime, but fifteen minutes prior to the deadline the Duke had not arrived.

Anxious looks began to appear on the faces of an Air Marshal, an Admiral of the Fleet and an Army General, but the Duke suddenly appeared on the scene. His arrival was rather special. He was passenger in an open top MG Sports car driven by a young Naval Lieutenant, without escort. The Duke was very calm and found time to talk cricket to the Bedsers before proceeding indoors. The broadcast went out on time... but only just.

An elite body of NCOs within the Branch worked as a Special Investigation Unit (SIB). Their work was invariably of a highly confidential nature. The men and women involved were hand-picked.

Five Region had its own detention block which frequently housed a variety of prisoners: some awaiting Court Martial or dismissal from the Service, or others due to be escorted back to their RAF Station.

An unusual desertion case arose involving an Airman who had been conscripted, but who after a few weeks in the Service had decided to desert.

NOBODY'S HERO

He was a British subject with a mid-European surname and thought to be of Romany origins. His Service record stated that he was a Gypsy and his home address had been given as an encampment near St Mary Cray in Kent. Together with a colleague I motored to St Mary Cray in civilian clothes. We decided to call at the local Police Station to see if they had any useful local knowledge to offer. We gleaned the information that the address we were interested in was on a caravan site which had become notorious as a place best avoided by the general public.

Notwithstanding the warning we decided to pay the site a visit... but we were to get nowhere. We located a particular caravan and were sure our deserter was inside, but a group of half a dozen rough-looking men would not let us close enough to do the job we had come to do. We decided that discretion was the better part of valour and left the site without our man!

We reported back to the local Police Station and they agreed to take out a Search Warrant and advise us when they had done so. A week later we returned to the site, accompanied by a Police Sergeant and a Police Constable, both in uniform. The 'reception committee' this time was even greater than on the previous occasion, but the Police Sergeant stood his ground and insisted on seeing the 'Camp Leader', a gypsy in his sixties. Following a fairly volatile discussion, the Camp Leader agreed that we could take our man with us, and after some lively to-ing and fro-ing, our deserter eventually emerged and we transported him back to HQ to await transfer to his RAF Unit.

He was later subject to disciplinary proceedings and given a period of detention at a special centre for more serious offenders. Within a month of his release he went AWOL (absent without leave) again...

My main recreational interest whilst in London was playing soccer for Five Region in a London based RAF League. Matches took place most Wednesdays, weather permitting, and the playing standards were high. Most sides had their complement of professional players and at one particular game our opponents fielded several international players including Eddie Hapgood, who was the then Captain of the all-conquering

Arsenal and England teams, George Male who was Hapgood's full back partner in the Arsenal and England team and Bernard Joy, who was also an Arsenal and England regular at centre half. Bernard went on to become the football correspondent for one of the leading newspapers.

We played this particular match at the Lyons (Cadby Hall) Sports Ground on a Wednesday afternoon. The referee, Mr A.J. (Jimmy) Jewell had refereed a pre-war Cup Final at Wembley, so it was quite an occasion. We lost by the odd goal in five after a game that we all recognised as a football feast. There were just five spectators present.

As an indication of the high standard of the Five Region team at that time we only needed to win our last match of the season to win the London League. We only managed a draw and finished runners-up.

My interest in Rugby Football was minimal, but my attendance as a spectator at two separate matches involving Service teams turned out to be distressing occasions. At a match between two RAF teams a player died during the game and the match was abandoned. At another match between two Army teams a player also died and this match was similarly abandoned – an unpleasant and unwelcome coincidence.

As occasion demanded, we were chauffeur-driven on some of our longer trips to the London fringe and our driver became a valuable part of our team. His rank was Leading Aircraftsman (LAC) and he always travelled in uniform. We knew him as 'Johnny'. Sometimes we wore civilian attire and were dropped at some distance from our destination. Johnny was reputed to have been the pre-war driver for an East End of London gang who carried out smash and grab raids, a story that was most probably true. He knew parts of London like the back of his hand and he was a superb driver. His manners and behaviour as an Airman were entirely beyond reproach; he was totally amenable to discipline and most of us regarded him as a thoroughly nice chap. Sometimes we sought his advice when tackling ticklish jobs and we never had cause to regret taking up his ideas as to how we should proceed. He was six feet tall, as strong as an ox and he was a useful man to have around particularly in some of the more notorious parts of London.

On only one occasion did he opt out on us and this was because the Airman we were looking for had been a member of a London gang which had been a rival of the group Johnny had been associated with. This particular 'villain' had been admitted to a well-known London hospital with injuries received during a fracas in a Leicester Square Night Club and information reached us that he was on the run from the Royal Air Force. We approached the hospital authorities, but they flatly refused to give information about patients. Purely by chance we were able to ascertain that our man was due to be released at a certain time on a certain date.

My colleague and I duly attended and took him into custody as he walked down the hospital steps on his way, he thought, to freedom. We confided in Johnny that we had made the arrest and he was a very relieved man. Johnny made the point that had he shown his face at or near the hospital the consequences for him could have been most unpleasant.

The extraordinary thing about Johnny was that if he had not disclosed his background to somebody, we would never have guessed what he had been in civilian life. In our view, he was admirably patriotic and a credit to the Service. For the period of the war, at least, he was a classic 'poacher turned gamekeeper'.

Early in 1943, an opportunity arose for personnel working at Five Region to volunteer for transfer to the 2nd Tactical Air Force (2 TAF), which was being formed as part of a special task force whose job it would be to invade Hitler's Fortress Europe. A number of us volunteered, and were transferred to RAF Bracknell, Berks – the newly formed Headquarters of the 2nd (UK) Tactical Air Force.

CHAPTER EIGHT

Preparing for the Invasion of France

Towards the middle of 1943, following service in the North African campaign, the RAF's 2nd Tactical Air Force (2TAF) became established at a base in the United Kingdom.

The Location: the country home of Miss Dorothy Paget, a wealthy racehorse owner, at Bracknell in Berkshire.

The Task : to provide air support for the Allied Forces in their campaign to destroy the German war machine and liberate the oppressed peoples of Europe from the tyranny of Nazism.

The AOC-in-C: Air Marshal Sir John D'Albiac. Air Officer Commanding in Chief, later succeeded by Air Vice Marshal Harry Broadhurst, a distinguished fighter pilot.

Emphasis from the beginning was on training and planning and men and women posted in 2TAF HQ became part of a massive training programme. After a period, specialised Security Sections were formed. I was promoted to Sergeant and given the job of leading a Team which came into being as No.6 RAF Security Section, 83 Group, TAF.

A few weeks later my overall superior, the Provost Marshal for 2TAF, Group Captain L.G. Brown asked me to consider taking a Commission, but after giving the matter very careful thought I decided that the opportunity to lead a team during the invasion of Europe was one that I did not want to pass up. Service on home bases in the UK was one thing, but I felt that I could not live with the thought that I would see my war service through without taking part in overseas operations. Deep down I also held the view that the real power in my new 2TAF environment lay with the Senior Non-Commissioned officers.

Miss Paget's delightful country home soon became a bustling military unit, surrounded by Nissen Huts and a tented encampment. The allotted task of No.6 Security Section was to provide field security support for 83 Group, 2nd Tactical Air Force as follows:

(i)   The security of RAF personnel, aircraft, airfields and equipment.

(ii) The removal from liberated territories of Nazi officials, collaborators and sympathisers.

(iii) The detection and elimination of subversive movements.

Security Section personnel were classed as non-combatants for reasons which I was never able to understand. As leader of the Section I was given wide powers and the Section was expected and required to fend for itself in the field. As occasion demanded, liaison with Army and Navy Intelligence Teams had to be maintained.

Full-scale field training operations took place at roughly two monthly intervals involving the Section in a portfolio of wide-ranging traffic and security activities in England and Scotland. One such operation entailed the road movement in convoy of a complete airfield from Scotland to the Bournemouth area, a massive operation lasting five days and nights in inclement weather. Well over a hundred vehicles were involved and the job required massive support from County Police Forces as we moved North to South.

Another highly specialised form of training for the Section took the form of Commando type courses at the RAF Station at Hartford Bridge (now Blackbushe Airport). These lasted two or three weeks and were extremely rigorous, covering every aspect of an infantry soldier's life in battlefield conditions. A limited number failed to stay the course mainly

---

Author's Note: At that time, the crack Free French Lorraine Squadron was operational from Hartford Bridge against targets in France. They were the first Free French Squadron to maintain regular sorties across the English Channel against their Homeland and they were a colourful, exciting group of individuals.

NOBODY'S HERO

due to their inability to cope with the physical aspects of the course. I was young and fit, but the physical exertions shook even the strongest. At the end of any given day I was almost on my knees with fatigue.

For part of our time at Bracknell we were under canvas in the grounds of Miss Paget's house and our existence was fairly spartan. Sleeping on straw filled palliasses in cold weather was a real trial and on occasion we slept in our clothes. Fortunately the messing arrangements were good and this helped to keep up our morale.

One particular user of the mess proved to be of interest because every so often he would sit at the breakfast table and open his morning mail… most of which contained cheques. He was a NCO whom I had previously seen teaching members of 2TAF HQ aircraft recognition, as part of a general training programme. His surname was Dennis and I was later to note that he sang the vocals at the Saturday night hop laid on for the Station at the Village Hall. On a particular evening, before he sang one of his numbers, the MC announced his name as Denny Dennis. We all knew who he was then. Denny was a widely acclaimed vocalist who sang with the top dance orchestras in the country. Pre-war he was often referred to as 'Britain's answer to Bing Crosby' and he was indeed a celebrity. Fame certainly hadn't gone to his head. He was a friendly, unassuming chap doing his bit for King and Country without fuss or bother.

After some weeks under canvas, we were allocated quarters in a detached house in the town of Bracknell, but this was only a temporary measure. We used the downstairs as office accommodation and the rest of the building as living space.

Off duty activities included cricket matches against other RAF units in the Home Counties area, we got together a useful side and won most of our games. Talking along these lines in a particular local pub led to a fair amount of banter from locals who played for Bracknell Village team. From all accounts they were an above average side and we had to face the regular taunt that we only kept on winning our matches because we were playing weak RAF sides. Word of this eventually reached one of our senior officers at 2TAF Headquarters and as a result I was summoned to his presence, not being sure what to expect.

The senior officer concerned turned out to be non other than (Wing Commander) P.G.H. Fender, a cricketing legend in his own lifetime, having played for Surrey and England. Without any beating about the bush he ordered me to get a cricket match arranged with the local team as soon as possible. And so it was that on a certain Wednesday afternoon two weeks later, RAF Bracknell cricket team arrived at the lovely village ground to play the village team. Contrary to my wishes, the Wing Commander made me Captain. I won the toss with his half-crown and put Bracknell into bat. I was able to open our attack with none other than A.V. (Alec) Bedser, the celebrated Surrey and England test cricketer. I was unsure as to where I should place PGH in the field so Alec Bedser suggested that I ask him where he wanted to field. I duly did this and with a wry smile on his face he replied, "You are the Captain, place me anywhere you like, as long as it's first slip!"

Alec Bedser got rid of the Bracknell batting quickly and their score was a modest one. The innings lasted just over an hour. I opened our batting with Eric Bedser, Alec's twin, also a Surrey and England player, and in less than an hour we had passed their total. The arrangements were then in a state of flux, but PGH suggested that as the match had been properly concluded we should leave. Someone took a photograph and we left.

That same evening we could not get to the pub quickly enough, but we were disappointed. The village team did not put in an appearance. One of the local wags suggested that they were out taking extra net practice.

A programme of major pre-invasion exercises was announced at this time and in order to enable us to provide the right kind of service, particularly on convoy work, we had to be able to perform to high standard on motorcycles. The fact that some of us had had only a limited pre-war experience meant that we had to put in a lot of hours in the saddle. Fortunately, there was precious little traffic on the roads, so we were not much of a danger to the public or ourselves.

Moto-cross type locations were used at the final stages and the *piece-de-resistance* was the Devils Punch Bowl, a custom built test arena near Guildford, Surrey. Successfully completing a circuit there was a test of anyone's skill and stamina.

The machines we started out with were 350cc Royal Enfields, but we were eventually equipped with the American Speed Cops machine, the 1,000cc Harley Davidson. This was motorcycle riding with a degree of sophistication! We were required to maintain and service the machines on a regular basis, and this we enjoyed.

We rode motorcycles most days, marshalling and shepherding convoys from one part of the South to another. We undertook the occasional sortie away from base and spent two to three days living rough on ad hoc sites under canvas. This was for the purpose of getting us prepared for the major assault on Europe. We slept on the floor and we ate rough and ready meals produced on spirit burners, sometimes not very successfully. A luxury, at times, was sitting at nights in a warm pub with a pint of beer and a packet of crisps, if we were lucky.

As the year 1943 progressed, pre-invasion training exercises took place in increasing numbers and on a more complex scale. We moved our operating base to a country house at Hartfield, Sussex, so that we were closer to the English Channel coast. One major aspect of these exercises was that of ensuring the safe movement of RAF units on to temporary airfields constructed in a matter of days on grassland normally used for agricultural purposes. The technique used involved the laying down of hundreds of yards of reinforced steel mesh sections on grass, and this proved to be highly successful. In next to no time fighter and fighter-bomber aircraft were landing and taking off as they would have to do in the wake of the invasion. RAF units sprang up in several locations in a matter of weeks. Our unit's main concern was to ensure that their road routes were clearly signed and that convoys arrived safely and on time.

The county of Kent saw several of these temporary landing strips brought into use and we spent a fair amount of our time in and around the marshes and the hop fields.

For one period we were sent on secondment to an Army Military Police Unit at Tunbridge for the purpose of enabling us to work more closely with them when a second front in Europe was opened-up. A secondary purpose was to provide them with the opportunity to work on our map reading capabilities.

This turned out to be much more demanding than we at first thought possible. On our first full day with them I found myself teamed up with an Army MP whose conveyance was a motorcycle. He spent some time discussing with me a 20-mile route we were going to take and he went to some pains to point this out on a very detailed Ordnance Survey Map.

I rode pillion to him and after every two miles or so he would stop, refer to the map, and ensure that I had absorbed what was taking place.

Part of the journey was made on roads which ran adjacent to the hop fields and were little more than country lanes. The exercise took a whole morning, it was thoroughly educational and picking the route from the map was more difficult than I had realised.

We returned to his base and after a pleasant lunch with him and his colleague, the Section spent the afternoon in a classroom situation absorbing further facts about the art of map reading. A chalk, talk and questions session, well handled by a Senior Army NCO. The following morning I teamed-up with the same MP, only this time the plan was different. The new arrangement was that I would ride pillion again, but this time I was to give the driver instructions as to which route he should follow. Furthermore, it was stipulated that he would only change direction when I specifically told him to do so. If I said nothing he would carry straight on. The only concession made was that I was free to tell him to stop as often as I liked so that I could consult the map.

At its furthest point our destination was fifteen miles away and the journey was expected to last two hours, allowing for stops. My MP made it plain that he was under strict instruction to give me no help at all.

We drove off and the whole thing turned out to be a near disaster for me. I kept making him stop whilst I read the map, then off we would go again. Some of my turns took us through the hop fields themselves, much to the delight of the hop pickers. The climax for me came when my directions took him into a farmyard where a goose leapt on to the tank of the motorcycle. Also, at that precise moment, a wasp appeared inside my goggles.

I yelled for a halt, by which time we were both in a bit of a state. The MP with the goose cradled in his arms and me with a wasp sting on the bridge of my nose! By the time we got back to base, an hour later, I was almost a physical and mental wreck. And the wasp sting was none too pleasant either. We had a good belly laugh about it in the mess that evening.

The map instruction and motorcycle sorties went on for a full week and by the time we left our Military Police hosts we had acquired a much better knowledge of the intricacies of reading a map in a country area.

The Army were very good to us from start to finish and there was obviously a value in exchanging views and details about the role we would play, jointly, when we landed in Europe.

Other pre-invasion training exercises on a major scale were carried out jointly with the Royal Navy in and around the coastal areas of Sussex and Hampshire, with Portsmouth, Poole and the Isle of Wight as areas of importance.

The initial stages of our involvement with the Navy were predominantly concerned with the technique of sealing motor vehicles so that they could operate in the sea, without drowning. Eventually we developed this to a fine art by the application to the engine of a magical plasticine type of substance which we called 'puggy'. The exhaust pipe was modified so that it ended up in a vertical position at least as high as the vehicle itself, thus preventing the engine from 'drowning'.

Having solved the vehicle sealing problems, we became substantially involved in mock landing operations from specially designed landing ships at Bracklesham Bay in Sussex and Poole Harbour in Dorset.

The Royal Navy, who were totally responsible for both men and vehicles, embarked the Section at Southampton Docks and then put to sea in the waters around the Isle of Wight.

The techniques necessary for loading landing ships were intricate and demanding particularly where this involved driving heavily loaded lorries up steep, narrow ramps in reverse gear. After a day or so at sea, to give us our sea legs, landings on the shore were effected and supervised by the Navy. The relationship between the two services during these exercises was first-class. On average, the Section spent two or three days with the Navy, on each occasion.

Initially, the actual landings were testing and on more than one occasion not everything went according to plan. A key tactic was to arrive off the beach at Bracklesham Bay around dawn. The ship would weigh anchor at some distance from the shore then slip in closer to the shore using the anchor cable. The naval Lieutenant in charge of the off-loading operation arranged for the lead to be swung over the side of the ship and when he was satisfied that the vessel was in the appropriate depth of water he gave the order for the first vehicle to be driven down a ramp which had been lowered in the prow. The initial drops were usually successful, the drivers having been trained never to touch the clutch and to concentrate on keeping the accelerator moderately depressed so that the vehicle moved forward on impact with the sea bed. Vehicles were fitted with four-wheel drive so impulsion was fairly immediate except when the vehicle landed in a seabed hole. Then there were problems, not easily resolved.

On one unfortunate occasion, the wrong reading was taken from the swinging of the lead and the first vehicles down the ramp ended up in six to eight feet of seawater. Even so, most drivers were able to make the shore and journeys of three to four hundred yards through the sea were quite common, the drivers coping with the problem by standing up whilst keeping contact with the accelerator pedal. The seabed at Bracklesham was ideal for our purposes.

Another off-loading hazard sometimes occurred after a number of vehicles had left the ship, thereby making the vessel lighter. The ship gradually eased back on the anchor cable away from the shore, the outcome was that the vehicles coming off last were dropped in deeper water. On one particularly disastrous day several three-ton lorries were seen moving out to sea with their drivers sitting on top of their cabs yelling for a tow. Some vehicles drowned but all the drivers were saved.

Once ashore a variety of activities intended to simulate landing conditions under fire took place. We captured Bracklesham on several occasions and failed to take Poole on another.

The training with all these exercises was demanding and tiring but being a sailor in the RAF had its compensations. The food was invariably good, the Navy's special woodbine cigarettes were a real luxury and the rum was of a quality unsurpassed. Providing the sea was calm no one had difficulty in getting to sleep.

These sea-going and landing operations increased in number in the early months of 1944 and the feeling grew that the 'big day' would probably come somewhere around June or July, 1944. The sudden availability of leave passes in the Spring of 1944 heightened the tension and in mid-May, all leave was stopped.

We, as a Section, eventually found ourselves encaged in a barbed-wire compound, along with a party of American infantrymen at a campsite at Hiltonbury, near Southampton. No one was allowed out and the buzz was that the invasion of France would take place in a matter of days. Meals were taken in the open or under canvas according to choice. The food again was excellent and there was as much beer as we could drink. The time was passed cleaning and servicing equipment, weapons and vehicles and playing 'brag', a card game which emptied the pocket surprisingly quickly — I never discovered why!

By the end of the first week, I, the Section Leader, was the only member of the Section not sleeping on a camp bed, so this I queried one morning over breakfast. Later that day, I too, had a camp bed, the acquisition of which came about due to the resourcefulness of some of my Section colleagues. Or so they said. The camp beds, they later admitted, were being "appropriated" from our American GI friends who must have known what was going on. Surprisingly, they did not create a fuss, but they did eventually take to securing their tents when they were leaving them to go on parade.

Apparently, with the breakfast discussion fresh in their minds, four members of the Section ventured out on yet another camp bed acquisition patrol, on my behalf, and in due course they came across a coloured American GI fast asleep on blankets on top of a camp bed. The intrepid four tiptoed up to the bed, took a corner of the blankets each and gently lowered the GI onto the floor. He did not blink or move and the bed was safely removed to my tent. The bed remained in my possession throughout the campaign in Europe but I never did fully accept their version of how they acquired it.

Towards the end of May I was given seven days leave and this I spent with my family. When I left my father at the railway station I wondered if I would ever see him again.

June 1944 came and it became obvious to us that the planned invasion of Europe was about to commence. The Section was on stand-by to move out at an hour's notice and this eventually took place on June 2nd. We motored as a Unit to Southampton Docks and were embarked in one of the largest landing ships, known to all as LSTs (Landing Ship Tanks). The vehicle deck in the vessel was huge and by nightfall it was full of tanks, half-track Self-Propelled guns, Bren-gun carriers, antiaircraft guns and soft vehicles, including those of No.6 RAF Security Section.

We put to sea in the dark and the movement of the ship was almost immediately noticeable. There was a swell running and most of us soon began to feel queasy.

We slept the night as best we could in or on camouflage nets on top of our vehicles, but none of us were relaxed. A disturbing aspect of being on the vehicle deck was that part of the vehicle complement was made up of tanks which moved from side to side with the movement of the ship.

Fortunately, the tanks were secured by huge chains locked into the ship's bottom, but even so they could move as much as two to three feet sideways and backwards. The sight of one of these massive lumps of steel coming your way was unpleasant and the noise of the steel tracks grating on steel was nerve-jangling.

We spent the next two days circumnavigating the Isle of Wight, at a distance, in the company of an increasing number of ships.

A typical anti-aircraft battery on the South coast of England attempting to shoot down German V1 flying bombs.

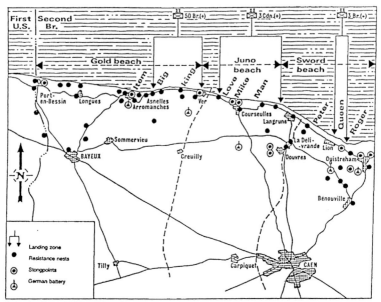

D-Day landings - British and Canadian sector.

A typical scene of devastation as troops pick their way through a Normandy town shortly after D-Day.

CHAPTER NINE

Operation Overlord

June 4th 1944 came in with a heavy sea running and our LST making slow progress just south of the Isle of Wight. Nearly everyone on board was seasick and the weather forecast was less than promising.

A feature of the LST was its round hull, so not only did it pitch but it rolled as well. By mid-day there were only a few men left on their feet and the waves were getting bigger. I lay on a camouflage net on top of a truck and hoped to die. There was no improvement as the day wore on, but towards evening the vessel was hove-to off the western end of the Isle of Wight and this made life a little more bearable.

June 5th started on a promising note. The sea began to calm down and the retching and vomiting gradually subsided. We ate our first cooked food and this brought about a noticeable improvement in morale. In the late evening an announcement was made to the effect that landings would take place in the morning on the Normandy coast. My orders for the Section were the 'Mike Green' part of 'Juno' beach.

June 6th was cold at dawn, but there was sweat on our heads and palms. Some of us were green from seasickness, but each of us was probably sunk in his own world of fear and anticipation. The atmosphere was electric, but the various groups aboard did their best to put on a brave face. The amount of laughter being heard was totally disproportionate to the occasion, a sure sign of the deeper emotional conflicts taking place. Most people had lain down the night before but no one had slept. Approaching 6 o'clock in the morning the huge prow doors of the LST ground open and the vehicle off-loading ramps were into position.

After a short interval, large flat-bottomed pontoons known as 'Rhinos' appeared and began taking on board the equipment and vehicles housed in the bowels of the LST. This was a very tricky operation, but eventually the Rhinos were fully loaded. The propulsion units for the Rhino were two powerful outboard motors mounted at the rear of the platform and manned by Army NCOs. The loading operation took the best part of an hour to complete and the Rhino then moved slowly away from the LST.

Overhead, hundreds of fighter and bomber aircraft zoomed towards targets on the shoreline. A combination of parachute and glider landings was clearly taking place.

The sandy shore of Normandy appeared to be about a mile away. In reality it could have been two or more. Between us and the shore we began to see the living and the dead in the water. The dead floated gently on the tide towards the beach.

A massive armada of Royal Navy warships, in line ahead, were blasting away at the Normandy shore with all the firepower they possessed. The task force was made up of hundreds of warships of all shapes and sizes, minesweepers, landing craft, merchant ships, block ships and miscellaneous support craft.

The Royal Air Force and the American Air Force had systematically attacked German airfields and installations for weeks before the assault began and our planes were actively controlling the skies overhead as we moved inshore. One of the important lessons that had been learned in other campaigns was the need for close co-ordination between Air and Ground forces.

The sight of battleships firing full broadsides was awe inspiring and one shuddered to think that their fifteen inch missiles would be hitting targets fifteen or more miles away. The scale and ferocity of it all was beyond comprehension. The noise level was unbelievable.

The Rhinos were stood off for a while awaiting landing instructions and this provided all aboard with a grandstand view of the opening exchanges of the greatest seaborne landing enterprise ever undertaken. The sea was literally covered with craft.

An LCT typical of those used for the D-Day landings.

The order to move inshore came and the Rhinos chugged their way towards the beach. The sea by this time was calm, but the water was cold. The passage to our landing zone on Juno beach was fairly uneventful, but suddenly an aircraft came out of the cloud and appeared to dive towards us. The anti-aircraft gunners on our "Rhino" were about to open up when they realised the aircraft was an RAF Mosquito making for the shore. The panic subsided and soon the off-loading ramps on the Rhinos were lowered. Vehicles began the drop into the sea and the final stage of the move to the beach began. The rising tide had reduced the gauntlets between the mine and wire obstacles on the beach to one hundred yards at the narrowest point and this made the final approach to the shore a dangerous operation. Perhaps as much by luck as by judgement I waded ashore on the 'Mike Green' sector of Juno beach at around 9am.

The bridgehead battles on the flanks were already one to two hours old. The 8th Irish Battalion of the Kings Regiment successfully carried out the initial assault on another section of Juno beach and sustained heavy losses.

The initial Allied Infantry attack on the Mike Green sector by Canadian troops had begun a few minutes before 8am and the Germans had responded with fierce determination. There were bodies in the water and on the beach, but a foothold had been gained. The casualties lying there were mostly infantrymen from the Royal Winnipeg Rifles. Juno beach was under heavy fire from artillery, mortars and machine guns. Those members of my Section not driving vehicles decided that the water was as safe a place as any so they jumped into the sea and I joined them. We waded the last two hundred yards to the shore, holding our rifles and Bren guns above our heads. A number of assault craft were lying on the sea bed, having been blown up by mines strung up amid a tangle of angle iron and stakes.

On the drive-in to the shore, one of the Rhinos carrying one of my Section Jeeps got entangled with barbed wire and metal stakes lower down the beach, attached to which were mines. There was an explosion; the Jeep and two of our colleagues sitting in it were thrown into the sea. They disappeared from view.

Once clear of the water I made my way towards the Beach Commander, a Naval Officer who was using a loudhailer directing the movements of those coming ashore. He raised the loudhailer and yelled at me, "What are you, combatants or non-combatants?" a question I had not really expected. After a very brief interval, during which I reflected on what I initially felt was an odd sort of question, I replied "Non-combatants, Sir." This was little more than an hour after the initial assault had gone in. The Beach Commander then instructed me to get the Section "dug-in" some fifty yards or so lower down the beach. Parts of the beach were mined and signed so we covered the ground in fear and trembling. Out came the spades, which were standard issue equipment and in next to no time we were below ground level. From our dug-outs we were able to observe the Beach Commander at work and this was indeed an impressive sight.

Over the Mike Green area of Juno Beach, he moved wherever there were Units about to land and he gave both advice and instructions to suit the circumstances. His main aid was the loudhailer, which never left his hand. He appeared to be completely unmindful of the risks to which he was continually exposing himself and during the hour or so he was in view to us, he did not actively take cover on one single occasion.

The pivot of his operations appeared to be a high section of tufted sand dunes which offered some natural protection, but he was on the move and involved to such an extent that he must have been living a charmed life. We assumed he had gone ashore with the first assault units. He was a brave man, by any standards, and it occurred to me on more than one occasion that he was actually revelling in what he was doing. He was truly a credit to the Royal Navy. An hour or so later the Beach Commander hailed us giving me a suitable landmark to aim for, a short distance inshore from the beach.

At that moment a Red Cross stretcher party came by carrying an Allied soldier whose arm was in a sling. He was smoking a cigarette and was smiling. I had written a postcard to my parents the previous night, so I popped the card inside the soldier's sling and asked him if he would get someone to post it when he got over to England. My mother told me some months later that she received the card at our Nottingham home in the late evening of the same day, June 6th 1944. I came to believe that someone had hand delivered it!

As we drove off the beach we registered the alarming fact that a team of four (British) Royal Engineers were busy with mine detectors on the stretch of land immediately adjacent to where we had been digging our holes just a short time previously. A fairly sobering experience during our first minutes ashore, made even more poignant as we drove past the pile of mines the Engineers had already located and removed. As we made our way inshore, we drove within yards of an infantry platoon, prone behind a nearby low wall, exchanging small arms and machine gun fire with German troops who had been left in a concealed position to harass invasion parties as they emerged from the beach. There was no let-up and the Germans were putting-up really fierce resistance over every piece of territory. Casualties were heavy on both sides. Smoke from burned-out buildings arose and the bodies of men lay under gas capes awaiting burial.

We progressed along a sand track in the direction of our target, the hamlet Graye-Sur-Mer and as we moved off the sand track on to a tarmac road we were staggered to see that as our last Section vehicle reached the road, an Army vehicle following immediately behind blew-up on a mine on the very track which we had just traversed; a second sobering experience.

We drove into Graye-Sur-Mer, pulled into the yard of a small farm, met the French occupants, and moved onto one of their nearby fields to establish a temporary base. They were totally bewildered by all that was going on around them.

We had achieved part of our first day's objective, we were content to dig-in under a sizeable hedge and put up our camouflage nets. There was

RAF Hurricanes (above) and Spitfires (below) flew endless sorties to provide D-Day air cover.

The USAF B-17 Flying Fortress played a key role in attacking enemy positions from the air.

The De Haviland Mosquito fighter/bomber, constructed entirely of wood, was also seen in the skies above the D-Day beaches.

RAF Wellington (above) and Lancaster (below) heavy bombers also pounded German installations prior to the D-Day landings.

NOBODY'S HERO

still a lot of small arms and mortar activity all around so it made sense to sit tight and take careful stock of our surroundings. Regrettably, there was no sign of our two colleagues who had been blown into the sea during the landing.

Some of the cattle from the farm lay dead in the field. They had been killed, we assumed, by shell fire from the off-shore naval barrage. A few beasts survived and they were milked in the open, that day, by the farmer's 15-year-old daughter, Jacqueline. She gave us milk to supplement our diet and she was delighted when I made her a present of a silver RAF brooch.

Single shot rifle fire, close at hand, indicated the presence of a German sniper who had obviously been left behind to carry out his deadly mission. To our relief, the following day he was eliminated by an Army patrol.

A senior RAF Officer, an Air Commodore, visited our campsite that evening and advised us to sleep the night under our vehicles as a heavy night of anti-aircraft activity was expected. We took his advice and when darkness fell the value of taking cover became quickly evident. The Luftwaffe was active overhead, but the Army and the Navy were ready and the barrage they put up was probably the greatest of the whole war. The sights and sounds were unbelievable and the result was that the efforts of the Luftwaffe were substantially diminished. At its peak the shrapnel from the anti-aircraft guns came down like rain and no firework display ever arranged could have compared with it. Anti-aircraft missiles dubbed 'flaming onions' were sent up in their thousands and the light from them at ground level was almost sufficient at times for one to be able to read a newspaper. In the hours shortly after midnight the Luftwaffe raids died away and we spent the rest of the night in our dugout, trying to fall asleep.

It had been a strange day and night on and off the beaches. I was both happy and relieved that I was still alive. Normandy was a dangerous and bloody place to be.

•

Luftwaffe pilots await the order to scramble (left). The greatly feared ME109E fighter (above) and a group of Junkers JU87 'Stukas' (below).

The Messerschmidt ME262A-1a, the first jet aircraft to enter squadron service with the Luftwaffe in 1945.

The Heinkel bomber, an all too regular sight over English towns during the Blitz.

CHAPTER TEN

The Bridgehead - Normandy

Activity on D-Day plus one began noisily at daybreak. Sleep had been limited; no doubt due in part to anxiety about what the next day would have in store for us.

One of our patrols went out early to carry out a general reconnaissance of the area, but as their Jeep entered a narrow lane they encountered their first German. They had travelled about two kilometres away from the farm, when they came almost face to face with a German Officer riding a motorbike. He braked instantly and they did the same, but before they collected themselves with a view to taking action he wheeled round and accelerated away at high speed, losing his cap in the process. I had little difficulty in accepting their statement that they had intended to take him prisoner and later on we had a good laugh about the incident. For the rest of the day, there was mild competition as to whose turn it was to wear the German's cap, but not outside our camp area. Getting shot whilst playing at being a German officer made little sense, but anything that eased the tension was welcome.

Later the same day, much to everyone's delight and relief, our two colleagues whose Jeep had been blown into the sea during the initial D-Day landings walked into our campsite little the worse for their experience. Their Jeep had been recovered from the sea and they had managed to get it back in working order. Their main problem had been to find us at the crowded bridgehead. There were a good many men wandering about the bridgehead during the early days trying to find their units. After being blown-up and plunged into the sea, they had clung to obstacles and debris on the tops of drowned vehicles. They were eventually picked-up by Army beach recovery squads and their Jeep was hauled ashore by Army engineers.

After putting up more tents and digging slit trenches, the unit stove was soon in action and we had refreshing hot tea to wash down the stodge of 'compo' rations. A standard compo (composition) food ration box, carefully used, could last the individual two days and porridge made from a small cube was probably the pick of its contents. Some swallowed the cube and allowed hot tea to brew the porridge in their stomachs – a not-to-be recommended dietary exercise!

By daybreak, a working party was busy making that essential field item, a latrine. A site behind a small group of bushes offering reasonable privacy was chosen. The latrine itself took the form of a pit about three feet deep and six feet long. Crossed poles cut out of a tree were installed, scissors fashion, at each extremity of the pit and a through pole was placed along the length of the pit and slotted between the end scissors. The through pole was fixed at a height that enabled the user to perch his backside over the centre of the pit. The compo ration box included toilet paper, so most of one's requirements were met. A bag of lime was placed adjacent to the pit for hygiene purposes. A simple hessian screen on stakes at the entrance to the pit made the operation acceptable and reasonably private.

One of our vehicles was a 2,000 gallon water bowser (tanker) so we were able to wash (and drink) in a fairly liberal fashion.

Part of the "field do's and don'ts" issued to us in the United Kingdom was an instruction not to drink local water as the Germans may have tampered with it. As a precaution, also, water purification tablets were standard issue in the compo ration box.

As we were clearing up after breakfast we noticed that, carefully concealed under camouflage nets at the opposite end of the field, were two half-track armoured vehicles that had not been there the night before. I made my way across and was greeted by a young Lieutenant from one of the armoured regiments. After exchanging the usual greetings he proceeded to explain that he and his Troop had run into difficulty the previous day (D-Day) by being attacked from the air. Originally there were five vehicles in his column and they we all carrying explosives. Their task had been to move across country and demolish certain railway facilities. They were carrying large, yellow identification flags spread across the roof of their vehicles, this being the agreed recognition sign for Allied Vehicles and Allied Aircraft. The five vehicles were several kilometres inland when an aeroplane strafed their small convoy and took out the three leading vehicles. An immense explosion made the narrow road they were traversing impassable so the two surviving vehicles turned back to await further orders. The Lieutenant mentioned that the "stuff" they were carrying would soon begin to sweat so he needed to be on the move shortly. An hour later the remnants of the task force drove South and West probably to deal with their next allotted target. I had previously asked the Lieutenant if they had been able to identify the aircraft involved in shooting them up and he replied, "Yes, it was American!"

By the time I arrived back at the dugout, a vehicle carrying four female nurses from the Nursing Yeomanry (FANYS) had pulled into our site. The lady officer in charge asked if they could camp with us for a while and we readily agreed. She explained they were awaiting other colleagues coming in via the Bridgehead, so we provided them with tea and helped them erect a tent. Their need for latrine facilities was explained to us and we arranged to share, subject to an arrangement whereby a piece of white cloth would be flown by them as a warning whilst they were in occupation.

The rest of the day was spent sorting out maps and equipment so that we could extend our security patrols the following day.

An unexpected development then took place. Team members found that whilst they were using the latrine someone was shooting at them, but apparently not with the intention of putting them out of action. The bullets being fired were hitting the pole on which the latrine users were sitting, causing it to vibrate. We decided to await further developments and these were not long in occurring. The FANYS officer had signified her intention of visiting the latrine and she had duly placed the white flag in position. A minute or so later she came charging out of the latrine carrying her pants in her hand. She had just been shot at whilst perched on the through pole. This then called for action on my part, so I lined up members of the Section, with their weapons, and ordered them to proceed at 10-yard intervals into a cornfield from whence the shots had been coming.

No one was sure what to expect, but suddenly a German soldier stood up about twenty yards away, levelled his rifle at the member of our team nearest to me and pulled the trigger, but there was no bang. We quickly overpowered the soldier only to find that he was a boy of no more than sixteen years of age. He proceeded to cry and when we examined his rifle we found it had jammed with a dud round in the breach. We took him prisoner and delivered him to the bridgehead where he joined a group of other prisoners awaiting shipment to the UK. The team member at whom the rifle had been levelled retrieved the dud round from the German's rifle as a keepsake and got down on his knees and prayed; a sight not likely to be forgotten. As a nightly event thereafter, he took himself to one side, sang a hymn, usually *The Old Rugged Cross* and spent time in prayer. I believe that one incident may have changed his whole outlook on life, from Pagan to Christian!

The following day the FANYS broke camp and moved on, having made contact with their colleagues via the Beach Commander. We were all very impressed with their composure whilst in a battle zone.

Our first casualty came about in the most unexpected way. One of my Section NCOs had entertained us quite often in pubs in the UK with his undoubted talents as a mimic, but upon landing in Normandy he began to imitate the various sounds made by shells and bullets and his performance soon became something more than a joke. Things deteriorated and in the interests of the other team members I had to tell him in plain language to stop the mimicking. This I found he was unable to do, and it became obvious that in the three short days we had spent in the bridgehead, his nerve had gone. I was at a loss to know what to do with him, but I managed to persuade him to stay in his tent while the other team members were in camp. I had more or less made up my mind to send him back to the UK when he took the matter out of my hands.

There was an explosion in his tent and when I went to see what had caused it, I found him holding a fairly large bullet cum cartridge in one hand with blood streaming from the other. It transpired that he had found the missile and was attempting to open it up for some unexplained reason using a nail and a hammer. It had exploded in his hand. We dressed his wound and drove him back to the bridgehead where he was taken over by Medical personnel.

This may have been a case of LMF (Lacks Moral Fibre) but it also serves to demonstrate the enormous psychological pressures on men in a battle zone. The nerves of some proved less strong than others. Obviously, it was a case of self inflicted injury, but with his nerve gone he was probably unaware of what he was doing. I had my doubts, so I took no further action, besides it was obvious that he would have been nothing more than a dangerous liability to myself and my colleagues in the days that lay ahead. There would be enough hazards to cope with as it was, so we were glad to see the back of him.

Later the same day, minor bursts of small arms fire continued to come from a clump of bushes about a quarter of a mile away from our site. Fortunately no one was hit. We returned fire with a Bren gun and after a second such response, the firing ceased. After an interval of about an hour I made my way over to the bushes and found the dead body of a German infantryman. I could not resist the temptation to find out who he was and a wallet in one of his tunic pockets soon provided the answer. The intrusion really left me little the wiser but a photograph in his wallet of his wife and two children shook me to the core. I beat a hasty retreat back to the Unit. The 'Rules of War' forbad interference with the dead and I carried my memories of the incident with me for weeks afterwards.

During D-Day+2 mortar fire was a constant source of worry and several times during the day salvoes of shells landed across the whole territory. This was made easy for the Germans due to work done by their surveyors during their years of occupation of the French Channel coast. Mortar emplacements had been arranged on pads at certain points, usually at road junctions, and surveyors had determined the distances involved between one point and another. This enabled the gunners to pinpoint targets to great effect. At one stage, by using field glasses we could actually pick-out the German mortar units at work, the ground interval between us at times being no more than two to three miles.

Later the same day we made a series of patrols in Jeeps, but achieved very little of security value. A usual port of call was the parish priest or the Mayor who could usually be relied upon to provide reliable information about individuals who had actively collaborated with the Germans during the occupation. It soon became obvious that most of those who were suspect had fled the area or were in hiding, so we were not over-committed as regards taking people into custody. We visited the local Gendarmerie and the local Doctor mainly to let them know that we were there and to confirm that we were preparing the way for the arrival of RAF units on French soil. Making the presence of the RAF evident on the ground in the battle zone was important, particularly for the Army who valued RAF support.

In one instance, the Mayor of one of the small communes was a local farmer and our visit to him very nearly got off the rails. He insisted on showing us his farm and in particular his liquor still which looked like nothing more than a huge vat sunk in a barn floor filled with a mass of rotting fruit, mainly apples. On the shelves on one side of the barn was a display of bottled wines and spirits enough to supply the whole village. His particular speciality was homemade Calvados – a spirit drink – that he served in tiny glasses no bigger than a thimble. This was a new drink to us and we made the fatal mistake of underestimating its potency. In next to no time we were 'in our cups' and it was thanks to the huge meal he provided that we managed to avoid becoming completely sloshed. After lunch he provided useful information about local people whose loyalties were suspect and he took great pride in telling us of his own experiences in the trenches in the 1914-18 war. He was later reappointed Mayor.

Work had already begun on farmland nearby to create an Advanced Landing Ground (ALG) for the RAF. It was the first of its kind in the British War Zone and it was built by an RAF Airfield Construction Group aided by the Royal Engineers and the Pioneer Corps. About thirty such ALGs were constructed in the War Zone.

The Airfield became known as B3. It was built under fire from German troops and became operational during the evening of June 9th, just three days after the initial landing on the beaches. An acceptably level surface was created by the use of bulldozers, graders and scrapers. Heavy steel mesh (Somerville Track) was then laid on the excavated surface. It was quick safe and effective. The week after D-Day 200 RAF aircraft had operated from B3, located at St. Croix sur Mer, a village only one and a quarter miles inland from the beach.

D+2 saw the arrival of British troops in the town of Bayeux, home of the famous tapestry. We apprehended and handed over to the local Gendarmerie a man and his son who had been actively collaborating with the local German garrison Commander. The night was fairly quiet and I slept properly for the first time.

D+3 was spent visiting the Mayor, the Gendarme and the Parish Priest at Creuilly, a small town lying west of our campsite. The Army Commander, General Montgomery was based at Creuilly with his famous Caravan. Some information about local collaborators was obtained, but those involved had either fled further inland to avoid arrest or were in hiding.

D+4 saw us making a second visit to the town of Bayeux. We made contact with an Army Intelligence Corps Unit and exchanged information. Field Security in the town itself was an Army responsibility, so our visit was undertaken for liaison purposes only. We were, however, given an opportunity to see a barbed wire compound guarded by British Servicemen. In it, we were told, were Servicemen who had declined to go into action against the enemy. Their future, we were told, was to be determined by Courts Martial in the United Kingdom.

D+5 involved us in a number of visits to French homes and businesses where there was evidence that individuals had actively collaborated with the occupying German forces. We took a man and a woman into custody pending further enquiries by the Gendarmerie.

Our return to base was accompanied by one of the most bizarre happenings one could ever wish to see. Liberator bombers of the US Air Force were returning over the Bridgehead from a sortie further inland. Suddenly one of the aircraft began a series of wild manoeuvres that were very threatening for those of us in its flight path. It became obvious that the aircraft had been damaged by anti-aircraft fire and that the crew had put it on automatic pilot and had baled out. For a period of about half an hour the aircraft performed all kinds of crazy manoeuvres, including diving and looping the loop: there was no telling where or when it might hit the ground. Finally an Allied fighter aircraft appeared and shot it down, much to everyone's relief.

The brothel at Bayeux was in demand and in use almost from the day the town was liberated. The 'hostesses' we were told had been brought under strict Allied medical supervision.

The Germans had not put up much resistance at Bayeux and the town was the first one of any note to come into Allied hands. Damage to property was relatively light, and the number of casualties sustained was less than anticipated.

Back at our campsite, one problem we were obliged to get involved with, but not from choice, was that of dealing with a dead body on the battlefield. The problem arose within days of arriving in the Bridgehead and I was at a loss to know how to cope with it.

A German infantryman lay dead near to the entrance to the field in which we had made our base. His steel helmet and his rifle were beside him. He was probably a casualty of the initial assault by the Army. The corpse was not obstructing our movements in any way, but after lying out in the hot sun it had swelled to such proportions that I feared it would burst and the smell was atrocious, as can be imagined. In addition there were dead cows in the same field, which were in a similar state of decomposition.

I had to take some action, particularly as regards the infantryman. Together with a couple of colleagues we approached the body with some trepidation; the swarms of flies all over the face, mouth, ears and eyes made my stomach turn over. He was a big man, probably weighing thirteen to fourteen stones, so moving him was something of a nightmare. I took the head and shoulders and my colleagues took a leg apiece. At each step we took, the gases in the body began to escape and this indeed was bizarre. There were noises top and bottom, and the stench was indescribably awful. We carried the body a distance of about two hundred yards and eventually got it onto a grassy bank alongside the road in shade. We drove the nozzle of the rifle into the ground alongside the body and topped it with his helmet. That was part one of the problem resolved. We then succeeded in getting the farmer to consent to removing the cows by means of a horse and cart. We gave him a hand with the job but the size and weight of the animals was more than we had bargained for and by the time the cows were on the cart we were beginning to feel the strain. As we walked away I could not help but register the sadness on the farmer's face. His living was based on milk yield and Allied shells had killed valuable members of his small herd, but he did not complain and he continued to supply us with eggs and milk.

The environmental improvement achieved justified the efforts we had made, but both jobs were particularly unpleasant, and neither of them had been catered for in our Training Manual.

The various political factions among the French population were active from the onset of military operations and delicate situations soon developed. The arrival of the Free French Leader General de Gaulle at the bridgehead during the early days of the invasion stimulated political activity. The General spoke from a soapbox in the town square at Bayeux and made a speech which was clearly aimed, in part, at the French people

---

Author's Note: The Prime Minister's original wish was to view the D-Day Landings from a destroyer off the coast of Normandy, but he was prevented from doing so by the King, who announced that if the Prime Minister were to go, he, the King would feel duty bound to be there at the head of his Armed Forces. In the event General Montgomery met Mr Churchill on the beachhead on the 12th June – D+6. From there he travelled about five miles inland to the General's Headquarters. My source – Winston S. Churchill II

in those regions of France still under German occupation. He returned to his UK headquarters shortly afterwards and the Allied authorities were pleased to see him go. This was clearly one of the first manifestations of his interest in becoming the next President of France.

D+6 was yet another day of patrols and visits and we made more arrests on security grounds. The highlight of the day took us all by surprise. We were driving back to our base towards lunchtime when the Prime Minister, Winston Churchill, accompanied by the Army Commander, General Montgomery, drove in a Jeep down the road to Creuilly where General Montgomery had his famous Caravan Headquarters. The road to Creuilly was clearly visible from German positions. This happening was a tremendous boost to morale but I think the risk the Prime Minister took, as leader of the nation, was enormous. By this time the bridgehead was only six to eight miles deep and there was combat activity everywhere. We got to within a couple of hundred yards of him and he gave us his familiar two finger Victory Sign.

Some idea of the magnitude of the assault on the Normandy coastline emerged when it was revealed that the embarkation ports for 'Overlord' stretched from Felixstowe on the East coast, the length of the South coast and the West coast round to and including the Bristol Channel. The overall plan involved the landing of 175,000 men, thousands of tons of stores, and 20,000 vehicles.

The build-up of men and equipment reached enormous proportions and the bridgehead was expanded to the East, to the South and to the West, but only after very fierce fighting.

The town of Caen, in particular, was heavily defended and the Army's attempts to dislodge the Germans were the subject of street-to-street battles that resulted in heavy casualties on both sides. According to the Allies plan, Caen, a vital road and railway communications centre, should have been captured on D-Day, but a month later it was still partly in German hands; indicative of the tremendous effort they made to retain it.

My Section moved into Caen on D+15 and set up office in a detached house that had been used until a short time previously by the German Army. Normal patrols in the Town were almost impossible because of heavy shell fire and street fighting. At one stage Canadian artillery units appeared at the rear of the house with their self-propelled Priest guns. They fired off heavy salvoes in quick succession and then withdrew. The Germans got the range fairly quickly and responded – and we suffered the consequences. Fortunately the house was well built and had a cellar that we used as a shelter. Unfortunately, some mattresses left behind by the Germans proved not to be so accommodating. We used them to lie down on and as a result half of the team contracted scabies.

Such was the strength of the German resistance that the RAF carried out a major bombing raid on the south of the town, but even this failed to achieve the required breakthrough. Some of their bombs were falling about a mile away from our billet and this gave us a few uncomfortable moments. That part of the town ended up flattened.

It was essential to keep the Section as active as possible and noteworthy happenings on the security front were visits I paid to a Convent in Caen where I met a senior male Catholic cleric who was introduced to me as Father Bob. He had been described as a valuable link with the French Resistance movement during the German occupation. I got on well with him, and we exchanged useful information. The battle for Caen, at this stage, was on a street-to-street basis. The element referred to by Father Bob was planned contact with a MAQUIS Unit (the French Underground Movement) with whom Father Bob had had regular contact throughout the German occupation. The Unit concerned had been active in the

---

Author's Note: There were four main types of resistance carried out by the French underground movement during the German occupation:

(i)   Collecting military intelligence.

(ii)   Running escape lines for Allied airmen who had been shot down.

(iii) Fighting the Germans by guerrilla warfare or sabotage of German equipment and installations.

(iv)   Political activity such as rumour mongering and general subversion.

'pipeline' by means of which Allied airmen who had been shot down over France were moved in stages across enemy-held territory into Spain and eventually back to the United Kingdom. French underground resistance units also carried out numerous attacks blowing up railway lines and sabotaging telephone systems.

Father Bob advised me that two key members in this Maquis chain would be arriving in Caen during the course of the next few days and his suggestion was that I should meet them. I agreed this would have a value and that I would be keen to talk to them. Two days later I received word from Father Bob that the two men had been shot up whilst trying to cross into the bridgehead and they were no longer in a fit state to complete their journey to Caen. Such were the perils faced by the men and women involved in the escape chain.

During one of my subsequent visits to the Convent I was speaking to Father Bob when a group of about 30 novice Nuns filed past us in one of the corridors and it was obvious that the presence of member of the Royal Air Force with a revolver round his waist caused the temperature to rise. Father Bob hastily reminded me that they were out of bounds to the RAF!

The Convent eventually had to be evacuated. Caen was a living hell, but nevertheless the nuns were reluctant to leave the people they tended in the community. The bombardment had shaken the heart out of the Town and evacuation made sense. The Royal Air Force played a physical part in the transportation of the Nuns by vehicles to a safer area.

During the lulls between the shelling in Caen we, on occasion, sat in the garden at the rear of the house, relaxing in the open air. We were sitting out there one day when a Canadian soldier climbed over the boundary wall and asked if we had any food to spare. He was somewhat dishevelled and had a nasty looking wound in the region of his left upper chest. We provided him with a clean wound dressing and gave him a meal, which he ate with some gusto. He did not have a lot to say, but we did manage to ascertain that he was out on sniping duties. This appeared to be confirmed by the magnificent rifle he carried, fitted with special telescopic sights. We pressed him to talk about his body wound and he explained that he had been hit a glancing blow by a bullet two days previously, the bullet having ricocheted off a steel shaving mirror he carried in the left upper pocket of his battle dress blouse. He still had the damaged mirror in his possession and seemed to think that the whole incident was hardly worth talking about. He seemed more concerned about an ankle he had sprained when he fell out of a tree when the bullet hit him, knocking him off balance.

When we pressed him as to whether he had achieved any 'success' with his sniping activities, he explained that a couple of days earlier he had taken up a position in trees on the outskirts of Caen. The land in front on him was a flat plain and German armour was coming forward in support of infantry fighting in the streets in the Southern half of the town. Canadian artillery, tanks and infantrymen were heavily committed in the battle for Caen. He spent a couple of hours from dawn onwards keeping watch, his basic task, he emphasised, was to pick-off German Officers.

Around mid-morning, a column of six German tanks approached along a road which, at its nearest point to his hiding place, was about six hundred yards distant. He loaded his rifle, released the safety catch and focused his telescopic sights on the leading tank. Almost immediately, the hatch lid came up and the head and shoulders of one of the occupants came into view. He was able to determine that the occupant was an officer, so he took aim and fired. The body in the hatch slumped forward and then disappeared inside the tank. He assumed one of the other occupants had dragged it down from the hatch. The column halted and the hatch on the second tank came up, so he repeated the process. This time the body was thrown out of the tank. He (the sniper) decided that two hits out of six was enough so he departed the scene as quickly as he could, satisfied with the morning's work.

Shortly after telling his story, he sloped off, back over the wall as quietly as he had arrived. He really was a mean, cool individual doing a highly specialised and dangerous job.

We stayed a few more days in Caen and fierce street fighting continued unabated. The town was battered to rubble but the Germans fought on in every building and shell crater. The people had either fled or were hiding in terror in what was left of their houses.

We were just about to start a patrol one morning when an Army Sergeant Major arrived outside the house and told us in no uncertain terms to clear out immediately as the Germans were in the next street and the Army wanted us out of the way. We left, as ordered, and made for the open ground adjacent to the airfield at Carpiquet. We left the road and set up a temporary field camp, awaiting developments in the battle for Caen. We had left some kit and personal belongings behind in Caen, but were able to recover these later on. By this time things had begun to calm down.

Good weather during the first two weeks of the invasion played an important part in helping the Allies establish the Bridgehead. Matters then took a substantial turn for the worse. On 19th June a hurricane-force storm, which lasted four days, severely damaged the man made (Mulberry) Harbour through which supplies vital to the Bridgehead operation had been arriving. Some 300 vessels were either beached or wrecked.

There were no established harbour facilities along the Normandy coastline, so a man-made harbour had been built in sections on the South coast of England. It was made up of a series of concrete caissons which were towed across the English Channel and assembled to create a sizeable pier alongside which supply boats could tie-up and off-load. Over two thousand caissons were needed to build the protective sea wall. Each caisson weighed six thousand tons. The man made harbour was nearly a mile long from the outer breakwater to the shore.

For a period of four days the storm prevented nearly all landing activity on the beaches and therefore interfered seriously with every operation; it was so fierce as to render offensive fighting extremely difficult. Conditions would have been ideal for a German counter offensive had it not been for the effectiveness of the Allied Air Forces campaign of isolation.

It took weeks of effort and ingenuity to overcome this massive set-back to the Allied Forces supply activities.

Caen finally fell to the British and Canadian Armies on July 9th. The losses on both sides had been heavy, but having broken the German defences, Allied troops began to pour through the Gap. The German army withdrew, but stood firm again in and around the town of Falaise, a few kilometres south of Caen. Here again the losses of men and tanks were enormous on both sides: 2,500 men were reported killed in the battle to establish the Bridgehead.

The subsequent 'Battle of the Falaise Gap', as it became known, proved to be a turning point, but the price paid had been dear. A breakthrough was eventually achieved and from then on the Army began to move out and across France. The German escape route from Falaise was finally sealed on August 21st, but by this time large numbers of German troops had already evaded capture.

The retreating German 7th Army were pounded by artillery and devastated by air attacks. There was great slaughter and 650 German tanks were destroyed. The armoured battle at the Falaise Gap was one of the major tank confrontations of the Normandy campaign. Normandy's narrow lanes and tangled high-banked hedgerows – the *bocage* – were death traps for men and tanks alike. It was touch-and-go for many days. Damaged and burned-out tanks were strewn along the roads, lanes and fields and there was clear evidence of heavy human casualties on both sides.

As we drove through the Gap, one particularly gruesome sight was that of a Canadian tank crew soldier who had tried to escape via the tank hatch. He was hanging by the legs, head down. His eyes were bulging out of their sockets, his mouth was open and several inches of his tongue were visible: a truly horrific sight.

We, as a Section, had been able to relax a little during the Falaise episode. We had continued with some basic security tasks, but were relieved when we were able to take to the open road, but our stay in Caen had been a terrifying experience.

Once the advance into open country began, it was part of our task to remain as close to the front as possible. At times, through our own errors, we found ourselves for short periods in advance of the line – not always a pleasant experience – and one patrol came near to a nasty ending.

We usually progressed from map reference to map reference, but the speed of the Army's advance made it difficult at times for us to know what they had captured and what they had not. We thought we were safe on this particular occasion, so we took a shortcut that fitted into the general route we had chosen from the map. We began the approach to a small village that was clearly shown on the map and everything ahead seemed calm. The villagers came out onto the street, cheering, and our small column was reduced to walking pace. Bottles of wine began to appear and the girls came into prominence. We eventually reached what looked like a crossroads at the centre of the village and it was here that we were due to take a left turn. The corner was 'blind' and I was in the leading Jeep, some yards ahead of the rest. We made the left turn and found ourselves facing the village square but here our progress came to a sudden halt. At the entrance to the square was a stationary German Tiger tank with its gun pointing in our direction. Members of the tank crew were on the ground alongside the tank and the moment they saw us they began to clamber back inside. This gave us time to reverse and beat a very hasty retreat. Even stranger still, the villagers cheered us on our way out with almost the same enthusiasm as they had shown on our way in! We eventually achieved our objective for the day via another route, without incident, and my decision not to try and capture the tank and its crew was probably one of the wisest I made during the whole campaign! But had I done otherwise and captured the tank, who knows, I may have become somebody's hero…

As we moved further and further across France, some security problems were posed by foreign nationals who had been brought to France by the Germans to work as slave labour during the construction of military fortifications along the coastline. Many thousands of individuals were rounded-up in the Eastern European territories annexed by Hitler and forcibly removed to France. When they were liberated by Allied Forces some wanted to return to their native lands, but others had more or less settled down in France. They had married French women and were content to stay where they were. Some of them had actively collaborated with the Germans, in occupation, so we had to root them out.

French women who had married German troops during the occupation posed a separate problem. Some of these relationships resulted in hostility being shown to the liberating armies and on one occasion, in the Bridgehead itself, two French women actually fired upon Canadian troops. The women were unceremoniously shot by the Canadians.

The work of our Section was eased when local residents provided information about those people who had been active locally in support of the Nazis, but care had to be taken to ensure that the informers were not using the security forces to settle old scores.

The presence of British subjects who had been living in France throughout the German occupation was also a matter calling for careful handling, but it was our experience that most of them were found to have remained loyal. They usually made themselves known to us and on no occasion were we required to take anyone into custody.

One particular patrol took a colleague and I into territory close to the town of Rouen where the Americans were active. We were driving along an A-class road (in our Jeep) at some speed when suddenly mortar shells began to hit the road in front of us. This really put the wind up us, because the shells were arriving from behind. My driver colleague pulled off the road immediately, the Jeep hit a concealed concrete stump with one hell of a bump and all three of us ended up in a ditch (i.e. the Jeep, my colleague and myself). We stayed put for a while and were glad to do so. We were both somewhat shaken and one of my legs was badly bruised. In addition, my colleague's false teeth had shot out, but he managed to recover them, intact!

From our position in the ditch we guessed that we were probably out of sight from whoever had fired the shots, so my colleague decided to recover the Jeep, which he discovered had been damaged at chassis level. As a precaution we waited another half hour or so then decided to drive on. We found that there was a problem with the steering, but we were able to struggle the vehicle along at about 15mph. We did this over a stretch of several miles and eventually came across an American Army Transport Unit. We stopped and asked for assistance and we really got it. Within the hour we were on our way again, but by this time my colleague was driving a brand new American (Ford) Jeep (our standard-issue Jeep was made in Canada). The American transport Officer said our Jeep was a write-off, so at his request we signed one of his forms and were allowed to take possession of the new vehicle. We just could not believe our luck. This was battlefield cooperation of the kind such as one could only dream about. The Americans thought it was all much ado about nothing. That day, the American Army demonstrated what the Allied cause was all about.

On our return to base our colleagues were suggesting that we could not have come by the vehicle by fair means, but we remained unmoved. The Jeep was to give us first-class service in the months ahead.

By the end of August, our main job in France had been more or less completed and the French authorities had not been slow to deal with those individuals considered to be a security risk. The RAF was dominant in the skies over our part of the war zone and the much-vaunted Luftwaffe was reduced to spasmodic hit and run raids. We had suffered just the one casualty and for this we were extremely grateful.

Our own supply position was good and food of a high standard had become available after the initial period of hard tack compo rations had ceased. We were also able to obtain some food from the countryside as we passed through; eggs and milk in particular. Wine and cigarettes were also in reasonable supply, but our bodies could have done with a decent bath. Freshening-up from a bucket of cold water was not exactly ideal and some of us experienced trouble with insects that seemed to like being inside our clothing. Being bug-ridden was thoroughly unpleasant, so we went in for shaved heads for a while. My own particular coiffure included a V for Victory centrepiece that made me look something like a convict in uniform, but I thoroughly enjoyed immersing my head in a bucket of water every morning.

Food in packs, alphabetically marked 'A' to 'E' became standard issue and there was variety in each pack. 'E' packs seemed to be the most sought-after because they sometimes contained steak and kidney puddings and peaches.

Progress across Northern France continued apace and the Army's sights were set on the Belgian border. On September 1st, the Guards and the 11th Armoured Division took Arras. On the 3rd, the 11th Armoured Division skirted Lille, leaving the 5th Division to clean up. On the 4th, the 11th Armoured Division were in Antwerp, but found the Germans dug-in on the banks of the Scheldt Estuary.

The Germans fought a determined rearguard action to delay use of the port to Allied supply ships. On the fifth, 50 Division, 12 Corps took Ghent, the first footing in Belgium. The Scheldt battle resulted in heavy casualties on both sides. It fell to the Canadians to bear the brunt in battles for Antwerp, the Scheldt Estuary and the stronghold of Walcheren.

In a five week period the Army took forty thousand prisoners and lost seven hundred officers and twelve thousand other ranks, killed, wounded, and missing. Of these, half were Canadians. Reviewing the Antwerp campaign, General Montgomery said later:

"I must admit to a bad mistake on my part. I underestimated the difficulties of opening up the approaches to Antwerp, so that we could get free use of the port. I reckoned that the Canadians could do this while we were going for the Ruhr. I was wrong".

Perhaps one of the outstanding and less pleasant aspects of our time in France had been the disappointment felt by the invading forces at the surly, off-hand attitude of a minority of the French people, particularly in the Bridgehead area itself.

There were exceptions, of course, but in the main we found the reaction of this minority to us hard to take and even harder to understand.

At tremendous cost in lives and materials, we were liberating their country from their traditional enemy, the Germans, but in carrying out this highly dangerous task, we were at times made to feel less than welcome.

From the onset we were conscious of the fact that in fighting the Germans and driving them out, we had damaged French farms and French property and had killed a lot of their cattle in the fields, but this surely was the price that had to be paid for liberty. There were, regrettably, also some civilian casualties.

Material considerations and the danger to which we had exposed them may in some measure have explained some people's attitude, but at the time the question was being asked: "Why have we bothered when they don't seem to want us here?"

On one particular occasion we had difficulty in persuading a small wine shop owner to open-up and sell us bottles of wine. We more or less had to bully her into doing so after she had made it obvious that she was not at all keen to serve us. We had French francs so it was thought not to have been a problem.

In general, the attitude of the civilian population took a variety of forms, not all of them negative. One prime illustration of this came about shortly after D-Day when a particularly attractive young French woman made her mark on us all by bathing in the sea off the Arromanche beach. The sight of this beauty in a bathing costume probably did more for the morale in that area than anyone realised at the time. She stayed for half an hour, then disappeared over the sand dunes.

The lady's intervention in the war may well have been carefully thought out, as a bit of fun or female bravado perhaps, but whether or not this was the case, there can be little doubt that in less than half an hour she had found herself several hundred admirers. And she carried it all off, beautifully – a real twentieth century 'Maid of Arromanche'.

The successful invasion of France had, however to be viewed against a significant new development in the technical conduct of the war: rocket warfare. The Germans had developed the V1 long range Flying Bomb, which to all intents and purposes was an unmanned aircraft. The first one landed on London on the 12th June 1944, just six days after the Normandy landings began.

Nothing quite like these rockets had been used previously by the Germans or anyone else as a means of mass destruction. Numerous V1s were launched at England, with London top of the target list. The rockets often appeared almost at rooftop height, sometimes careering erratically across the skyline. Their gyro steering mechanism was unreliable and quite frequently the missiles went off course and out of control; a number of them appearing over parts of the South of England, obviously flying erratically. The rocket's propellant motor was designed to cut out over its target causing the missile to dive to the earth in the form of a huge bomb. The drone of the rocket motor became immediately identifiable and had a serious effect on morale. For those in the rocket's flight path the moments following the cut-out of the motor were terrifying. The ensuing explosion occurred after about a fifteen second interval and the damage done over a wide area was colossal. These rockets flew at an operational height of two to three thousand feet and achieved speeds of up to 400mph.

At one stage V1 launches were 120 a day, but on June 15th, 1944, 245 missiles were launched from 55 sites in a 24-hour period. By the end of the month 2,000 V1s had been launched against London. Allied anti-aircraft and fighter aircraft units had great difficulty in coping with them. People in England referred to them as 'doodlebugs', but they were a lot more deadly than their nickname made them sound; the German name for them was *Vergeltungs Waffen* (reprisal weapons). Obviously they were the German response to the heavy bombing of their country by the Allied air forces. But worse was to come.

The VI was followed by an even more sinister weapon know as the V2 Rocket. This was fired high into the atmosphere and did not develop the aircraft flight pattern of the V1. It was, therefore, virtually impossible to detect or destroy.

The first V2 landed on London on August 1st 1944, and its effect was devastating. The V2 was particularly destructive when it fell directly into a structure of some kind. Owing to its speed, it penetrated deeply into the ground and its great explosive effect was exerted directly upwards. As a consequence, when it fell into open spaces it was relatively ineffective, but so great was its explosive charge when it hit a building that destruction was almost complete. V2 rockets were 46 feet long and weighed 12 tons. The rocket motor ran on alcohol and liquid oxygen. They achieved a speed of 3,600mph and reached a height of 100,000 feet and were launched from a platform towed by a truck.

In terms of lives and materials the cost of the Normandy campaign had been high. Figures quoted at the time gave German losses as being 200,000 killed or wounded and over 200,000 taken prisoner. Two German armies were annihilated in the battle of the Falaise Gap alone. German material losses were said to be 1,800 tanks, 3,000 guns and 20,000 vehicles. Allied casualties were 60,000, of whom nearly 9,000 were killed, but the situation could have been worse. Had the German defences on the Normandy coast been contiguous, the British casualty figure would undoubtedly have been much higher. In considering Allied losses, account had also to be taken of the fact that the Allies had absolute command of sea and air, enabling them to establish the Bridgehead from which they were not eventually in danger of being dislodged. Had this not been the case Allied losses would undoubtedly have been much greater.

Paris fell to a joint American/French spearhead force on August 25th, 1944, and this was a tremendous boost to the morale of Allied troops. The liberation took place without too much trouble. To his credit, the German General in charge of the Garrison refused to raze the city as ordered and withdrew his troops.

News of the taking of the City had an adverse effect on the morale of German troops and the German population as a whole, of this there can be no doubt.

On July 20th, 1944, an attempt by a dissident group of German officers to kill Hitler failed. A bomb was placed under a meeting table in the Reich Chancellery, but when it went off Hitler escaped with only minor injuries from which he subsequently recovered. He had the plotters quickly put to death.

The crushing defeat of the Germans in Normandy was followed by orders for the Allied armies to keep moving forward as fast as was possible. The new goal was the river Rhine in Germany and no longer the river Seine in France, but steadily increasing German resistance, bad weather and supply problems combined to impede the Army's progress.

Extended supply lines from the temporary harbour in Normandy became a major problem. Bringing up petrol, ammunition and food by a road transport operation dubbed 'The Red Ball Express' was far from ideal. Troops could manage adequately on emergency rations, but without petrol, the vast amounts of mechanical equipment, planes, tanks and other vehicles could not be kept moving. It was five months before other ports came into use and this took its toll.

The Germans everywhere were withdrawing, but they continued to use their armoured divisions to slow down the Allied advance. There were frequent, vicious engagements, but these encounters were usually short-lived. The advance became a motorised chase with everybody riding on whatever means of transport and mobile weaponry that was available towards Germany's main defence bastion in the West – the Siegfried Line, a system of pillboxes, tank traps, and strongpoints stretching the length of Germany's Western frontier. It was built in the 1930s and was said to be impregnable. However, the French equivalent, the Maginot Line, also built in the 1930s and stretching the length of their Eastern border with Germany had been easily breached by German *blitzkrieg* tactics in 1940.

The summer nights seemed short and there was little time for sleep. Eating, re-fuelling, servicing vehicles and weapons meant that there were not enough hours in a day to accomplish all the tasks that were necessary. Most of us were becoming red-eyed and beginning to feel the strain. The RAF was busy overhead the whole time, providing an umbrella of fighter-bombers, and this substantially assisted morale on the ground. Rows of destroyed German vehicles and equipment provided ample proof for advancing troops of the excellent job being done by the pilots.

Adolf Hitler's *Lebensraum* (living space) plans were really falling apart. In addition to his annexation of Holland, Belgium and France, he wanted Russia's industries and agricultural lands and even though he had signed a non-aggression pact with Russia in 1939 he finally launched his massive military machine against Russia in the summer of 1941. The assault was code named 'Barbarossa'. Hitler's forces rapidly conquered huge areas of the Soviet Union and at one stage they were in sight of the Russian capital, Moscow. But the fierce Russian winter and the implacable Russian spirit proved to be the German's undoing. Stalin, the Russian premier, mobilised a massive army and counter-attacked. They gradually recaptured all the territory that had previously been lost. The counter attack became a rout and the Russian army moved inexorably towards East German territories whilst at the same time the Allied armies set their sights on Western Germany.

❖ ❖ ❖

The Russians lost over 20 million men, women and children, killed and wounded during the campaign against Hitler's armies. During my post-war service as an Intelligence Officer in Germany, I was allowed the services of a Batman (an Officer's servant). He had been a machine gunner in the German Army and had fought on the Russian front. One day I asked him how many Russian soldiers he himself had gunned down and his reply was, "at least a thousand". When he worked for me he was only 22 years of age. What a beginning for a young man's adult life!

CHAPTER ELEVEN

Belgium, 1944

The terrain we traversed in Belgium was flat, open and unwooded and well served by major roads. The battlefields of the 1914-18 war were crossed in a matter of hours and conjecture that the war would be 'over in weeks' was frequently heard.

Crossing the frontier from France was particularly noteworthy because of the friendly attitude of the Belgian people.

From the very first days that Allied Forces entered their country, the Belgians came onto the streets to welcome us as liberators in a very positive and heart-warming way.

All their doors were opened and what food and drink they possessed was placed on tables outside the front of their houses. We were encouraged to help ourselves. Spontaneous street parties were quite common and we were almost obliged to join in. Flags were being waved, the women were embracing and kissing everybody and the happiness of the people was there for all to see.

At times their enthusiasm temporarily stopped troop movements, so we just sat in the vehicles and enjoyed what was going on. The women and children climbed onto and into our vehicles and they gave the impression that wherever we were going they were going too. It was all very pleasant and it helped to ease the pressure on us.

These contacts with the people had the effect of re-charging our batteries, but once out of the towns we had to resume the posture of total vigilance and this was difficult after having been so relaxed. The Germans were fighting fierce rearguard actions as the Allies got nearer to their homeland and in the remote areas that had been bypassed by the main Army thrust, there were sizeable pockets of troops still fighting on.

The element of surprise gave these rearguard elements a considerable advantage and, being skilfully concealed as they often were, they were a constant source of worry and danger. Fortunately for me, none of my men became their victim, but we had some narrow escapes.

Almost coincidental with our arrival in Belgium, the emergence of a black market between Forces personnel and the civilian population necessitated action on our part, particularly where the item being traded was petrol intended for use on military operations. Units carried their own supplies so there were opportunities for troops and the civilian population to trade. Money was a means of exchange, but bartering petrol for wine, and occasionally women, was fairly common. Chocolate and cigarettes were other commodities, but these were legitimately the property of the troops, so a blind eye was turned to these transactions.

A lesser-known but equally important type of security activity involved us in the location of women who were suffering from venereal diseases. It was inevitably the case that women and troops got together, and for troops who assumed that there may be no tomorrow, caution was often thrown to the winds. The supply of effective prophylactics was a problem for forces on the move and a number of servicemen contracted sexually transmitted diseases. It was quite often the case that women were throwing themselves at the troops without a lot of ceremony, and not all of them were free from infection.

Later on we were interested to learn that the Germans dealt with this problem by having brothels under the control of their armed forces. The women staffing the brothels were under constant medical supervision and in some instances were actually enrolled in the armed forces. As a result, sexually transmitted diseases were less of a problem for them.

As opportunity presented itself, films emphasising the problems caused by sexually transmitted diseases were shown to the troops and these had a salutary effect, if only for short periods of time.

Problems caused by lice and bugs were also common, but basic hygiene and first aid was usually sufficient to prevent infestation becoming a major problem. At one stage I was lousy myself, but I put the problem to rights by dowsing the insects with high octane petrol. My skin took it badly, however, and removing the bugs, particularly from the more sensitive parts of the body, was a particularly painful process.

But the major problem for everyone was that of keeping one's nerves under proper control. Some of our forays into country areas were nerve-racking and even birds spooked out of hedgerows and trees often made one's hair stand on end. At other times the silence could seem deafening and quite frightening. An odd thing this, but we came to believe that silence was the harbinger of danger.

One journey made between two small towns took us onto a second-class country road. A hump-backed bridge came into view, obviously over water. We could not see what was on the other side, so we approached it cautiously. I went ahead on foot and as I moved onto the bridge approach itself I could see, on the other side, an anti-tank gun pointing in the direction of the bridge. It was placed about twenty yards away. At first there appeared to be no signs of life, but a German soldier limped out of the hedge and sat himself on the frame of the gun in the firing position. I tiptoed back to our Jeep and explained to my colleague what I had seen. We decided to take a flier at the bridge. We had the German outnumbered two-to-one and his chances of getting a shot away quickly enough to hit our speeding Jeep were close to zero. We hit the bridge entrance at speed and in next to no time we were alongside the anti-tank gun.

The German just sat there, amazed, and it was obvious that he posed no threat to us at all. The Sten gun pointing at him, no doubt helped. We could see that he was only a youngster and when we later checked on his age he said he was sixteen. He remained seated on the gun but we noticed that he wore a boot on only one of his feet. We also noticed that the sock on his other foot was bloodstained from what looked like a sizeable wound. We soon realised he was both terrified and in some pain and after a struggle we managed to remove the bloodstained sock, revealing an ugly shrapnel wound three or four inches long. The wound itself was oozing pus, so we carried out our own first aid by dousing the foot with an antiseptic and squeezing out some of the pus. We applied a standard field dressing, swathed the foot in a bandage and put his boot back on after cutting away most of its upper part. We then gave him tea to drink and loaded him into the back of our Jeep.

Curious to know what had gone on before we arrived at the bridge, my colleague made it his business to obtain the German's story as we drove along. Apparently, he and two other Gunners had been positioned at the bridge the previous evening to await the arrival of British vehicles and/or tanks. Darkness came and they all lay down to sleep the night beside the gun. When the youngster woke up in the morning the other two Gunners had flown. He said his foot injury had been sustained when they ran into shellfire during a previous skirmish. He added that this had happened some days previously. We hung onto him until we were able to hand him over, as a prisoner, to a RAMC (Medical) unit later that morning. When I last saw his face there was a trace of a smile on it. We then got back to duty. I was in no doubt that he was glad the war was all over as far as he was concerned.

The City of Brussels was our next main destination, but there was work to be done before we got there.

A patrol began after breakfast one morning and the plan was to visit the parish Priest and the Mayor of a town on our route. There had, of course, been Belgian collaborators throughout the German occupation and we were checking on these and other security matters.

We were about three miles short of the town when we noticed a man with what appeared to be a white cap on his head whistling and signalling from across a field. He appeared to be carrying a bag in his hand and he was limping slightly.

We stopped and waited and when he got nearer we could see that he was wearing RAF uniform. This puzzled us for a moment or two, but we then realised that the white cap he was wearing was a head wound dressing and the 'bag' he was carrying was his flying helmet and goggles. He was also wearing flying boots and the rank ribbon of a Flying Officer; obviously he was one of us. We sat and smoked a cigarette with him whilst he explained what had happened to him. He said he had been one of a flight of six fighter/bomber aircraft out on a mission and as he came out of cloud his machine was hit by a burst of machinegun fire from below. To both his surprise and amazement he saw that an aircraft carrying American markings had shot him up. His engine had been put out of action, but he was able to 'pancake' the machine onto a nearby grass meadow. On hitting the ground he had hit his head on the canopy frame with a substantial bump, causing some bleeding. His leg had also taken a knock at the same time, but otherwise he was all right. The dressing on his head turned out to be the white scarf he had made a habit of wearing on sorties.

We were able to deviate from our route and drop him safely back at his airfield an hour or so later. We concluded that being shot at by 'friendly' aircraft was apparently not the least of the hazards RAF fliers had faced from D-Day onwards. Back at his base our Flying Officer told us that a colleague of his held their squadron record for 'shoot-downs', having been shot down by the Americans on two consecutive days.

Some days later, by an extraordinary coincidence, we came across another Airman, walking along a country road, but his circumstances were quite different. This time we were on patrol, seeking out a local French politician, when we noticed, some way ahead, a man walking along the grass verge. As we got nearer to him we could see that he was wearing RAF uniform carrying the ribbon of Pilot Officer. We stopped and asked if he wanted a lift somewhere, but he, having noted that our Jeep was carrying the sign "No 6 RAF Security Section~, said he felt he ought to explain what had been happening to him before he did so. Out came the cigarettes and we sat in the Jeep and listened.

He began his story by explaining that some eighteen months earlier he had been part of a 'plane crew operating over Belgium. The aircraft had been damaged by anti-aircraft fire and the crew had been ordered to bale out. He had done so and had landed without injury or incident in a grass field. He carried out the official drill of burying his parachute and he then settled down in the hedgerow. It was late evening and when darkness finally came he lay in the hedge and slept. When dawn broke he could see that he had landed on farmland with the farm buildings about a mile away. He knew he was in Belgium, so he began to consider what he should do next, realising that he could not stay holed up in the hedge indefinitely. He stayed put for some hours and changed his mind a number of times as to what he should do. His mind was still in a state of flux when he heard the sound of a horse and cart coming up the lane at the back of the hedgerow in which he was hiding. He peered over the top and saw that the person in the driving seat of the cart was a woman. As the cart got nearer to him he could see that she was probably in her twenties. She was wearing a shirt and trousers and her appearance told him that she was probably a working member of a farming family.

He made up his mind that this development provided him with an opportunity to do something so he waited until the cart was a few yards away, then he stepped out of the hedge into the path of the horse. The young woman was obviously startled but she had the presence of mind to pull on the reins. The cart stopped, the young woman then appeared to be getting ready to make a run for it, but she stayed put in the seat and made no movement at all.

The officer smiled at her and said in his schoolboy French, *"Je suis Anglais"*. The young woman said nothing, but she was obviously weighing-up the unusual situation in which she found herself. After what seemed a long pause she replied *"Venez avec moi"*. She beckoned for him to climb on to the back of the cart and this he did. The young woman drove the cart to the farm, up to a barn, opened the door, and drove the horse and cart in with him still in the back. She indicated that he should climb a ladder into the loft and this he did. She then uncoupled the horse and led it out of the barn. He sat down on some hay and began to wonder what was going to happen to him next. He did not have long to wait for an answer. Through the barn door came a man whom he assumed was the young woman's father. He was accompanied by a woman, probably the man's wife and the woman driver of the cart.

The man was carrying a shotgun, but he did not look very threatening. The young woman then asked him in fairly good English to come down and to his relief and delight both the man and his wife greeted him with a smile and a handshake. They spoke no English, but the young woman, who explained that she was their daughter, obviously did. At the Farmer's suggestion they left the barn and went into the farmhouse. There they sat down at a table and a bottle of wine was soon produced. Aided by hand signals in the direction of the man and his wife and the young woman's reasonable knowledge of English he explained how and why he had come to be hiding on their farm. He sensed he had struck lucky and had made a wise decision in showing himself. At the table it was agreed that they would hide him in the barn at least until the Germans had stopped searching for the crew of the aeroplane. He slept in the barn and the family brought him meals and drinks regularly. They took him for short walks when darkness came.

The days and weeks passed without incident and, as the farm was remote, he came to feel he was in safe hands in a safe place. The young woman spent some time talking to him as she delivered the food and this he found very pleasant. As time passed he was allowed to come out of the barn during daylight without taking risks. The consequences for the Belgian family would have been severe had the Germans found out that they were hiding a British airman. They would probably have been shot.

Complications began to set in as he realised that he and the farmer's daughter were attracted to each other. A romance gradually developed and the farmer and his wife became aware of it. The two young lovers spent more and more time together and the situation got very complex because he was already engaged to a young woman in England – a fact that he did not disclose to his Belgian companion. Nevertheless the romance continued. The liberation of Belgium being at hand, he eventually told a distressed family that he would have to leave them and return to the Royal Air Force. Radio broadcasts had already been made across the liberated territories advising aircrew who were in hiding to present themselves to any unit of the Allied forces and to seek assistance. After a few more days of anguish and tears he had left his young French lover and her parents, promising to write. He had then taken to the open road where we came across him. We found his account of his time with the family so moving and it took my colleague and I some days to get it out of our minds. We drove him to a RAF unit and left him there.

During another patrol the following day colleagues were travelling along a minor road in the country when, through a gap in the hedge 100 yards or so ahead, a platoon of German soldiers suddenly appeared. My colleagues were about to move into action when they noticed that following the platoon out of the hedge were some British soldiers who had just taken the Germans prisoner. Subsequently, we treated the incident as a joke, but had the British soldiers arrived on the scene a few seconds later than they did, my colleagues might have found themselves embarking on a course of action that could have had serious consequences, particularly if they had opened fire on the Germans who were already prisoners of war.

A third incident was concerned with a Messerschmidt fighter aircraft that was brought down by anti-aircraft guns as a colleague and I drove down a lane between fields. Smoke was pouring out of the aircraft's engine when it came into our view and we could see the pilot fighting to get the plane down in a field to our left. He succeeded in doing so and jumped out of the cockpit apparently unhurt. We stopped our Jeep and made our way through a hedge in the direction of the plane, but when we were about two hundred yards away the pilot pulled out a revolver and fired shots in our direction. We hit the ground and were about to return fire when he threw the gun away and put his hands up. We took him prisoner and put him in the front seat of the Jeep. My colleague drove and I sat behind keeping an eye on our prisoner. We drove on, and in about half a mile we came to a bridge across a small river. Positioned on the bridge was an anti-aircraft gun manned by American soldiers. They were actually

---

Author's Note: The Belgians hid and cared for a number of Allied airmen during the German occupation at great personal risk to themselves. Those who were detected were often shot.

in the process of cleaning the gun so we jumped to the conclusion that this was the weapon that had brought the German plane down. The Americans were somewhat taken aback when they realised who the man sitting next to the driver of our Jeep was, and for some minutes there was a good deal of excitement. We explained our part in the pilot's arrest and it was obvious that their gun had done the damage to the plane.

We were asked by the Americans to stay for a meal and an excellent meal it was. They were cock-a-hoop about their success, their first, and they asked us to make a written statement detailing our involvement in the incident. Somewhat to our surprise, the statement had to be entered on a form, which we both signed.

The Lieutenant in charge explained that the report would be transmitted to their base in the USA and their success would result in the unit receiving extra benefits in kind in recognition of their success. We did not fully comprehend what this meant, but we took it to mean that it was all part of some kind of bonus scheme whereby their achievements were rewarded with creature comforts from the USA. We left the German pilot in the Americans' hands and they were pleased to have him as their prisoner.

The advance halted in phases whilst the Army carried out mopping-up operations. During these lulls we continued routine patrols and some of these had their interesting moments. On one occasion I set off on patrol intending to visit the Mayor of a fair sized town that was close to the border with Holland. There were two of us in a Jeep that carried a Bren-gun mounted on a tripod on the vehicles bonnet. My colleague was the driver and I was the map-reader. We knew we were near the front because we could hear loud gunfire, particularly that from light artillery. The roads we were traversing were third or fourth class and we were soon out in open country. After twenty minutes or so I had to admit I was lost, so we came to a halt.

There was a farmhouse ahead and we drove slowly towards its entrance to seek instructions as to how to get to our destination. As we were almost up to the farmyard, a man appeared and he began to reach for something in the pocket of a coat he was wearing. Having been schooled not to take risks, I knocked the safety catch off the Bren gun and the driver braked. Nothing untoward happened, however, and the man, who turned out to be a goodly age, sauntered up to my side of the Jeep and pulled out of his pocket a big ear trumpet; it must have been a foot long! He turned his head to one side and placed the instrument to his left ear. I took hold of the bell end of the device and started shouting into it in my schoolboy French, *"Pouvez-vous m'indiquez la route, etc, etc"*. The old man gazed up at me with an innocent, blank look and I soon realised that effective contact had not taken place. By this time my colleague was into the belly laughs and I found it impossible not to join him. It was all of ten minutes before we recovered our composure during which time the old man sloped off, probably wondering what it was all about.

We then pulled into the farmyard and the son of the farmer put us right as regards the road we should have taken. Had the old boy pulled out a gun when he dived into his pocket the outcome could have been very different. I quietly thanked God afterwards that he hadn't. As it was, we still had tears of mirth in our eyes as we continued our journey.

One of the national slogans found everywhere in the United Kingdom during the war was "Careless talk costs lives!" and the civilian population were continually warned to be careful who they talking to and what they were talking about.

As regards men and women in the Armed Forces it was also considered necessary and advisable that they should exercise caution particularly as regards letters being written to relatives at home. Censorship of Services mail took place, on an extensive scale. In those instances where letters were considered to be giving away vital information about Service activities, the offending letter was edited and a copy was passed to Security Sections such as mine for action. One of our duties was to visit the Unit and speak to the letter writer about his or her indiscretion.

As time went on it became obvious that individuals were prone to putting operational details into letters and this had to be stopped in everyone's interests. I handled a number of these intercepts and the extent of my action was usually to caution the individual concerned. Invariably one warning was sufficient. A second offence would have been considered a serious breach of discipline.

One particular intercept reached me during the campaign in Belgium and it was a clear instance where a fighter-bomber pilot in a letter to a friend in the UK was being a bit too explicit about Squadron activities in the battle zone. He was a member of a forward Typhoon Squadron and I eventually located his Squadron on a temporary airfield where sorties against the enemy were being undertaken from dawn to dusk.

I contacted his Commanding Officer, on site, and he explained that the particular pilot I was seeking to talk to had taken off on his second mission of the day against the enemy. I had no option but to await his return from the mission.

After an hour or so had elapsed it became obvious that he was not coming back. I took my leave of the Commanding Officer, feeling substantially subdued and not at all sorry that my mission had not been accomplished.

Another intercept caused quite a stir among us because it came into the classification of being "pornographic" and the authorities wanted it dealt with. The details were explicit by any standards, but I believe my interview with the writer was sufficient to cause him not to commit such matter to paper again. The letter had been intended for his fiancée in England, but he agreed it would best be destroyed. The shock of being told the nature of my visit was such that he almost passed-out on me.

At any time, this censorship duty was one of the most unpalatable, but necessary jobs we were required to undertake. We kept our feelings under control by recognising the indisputable fact that careless talk did cost lives.

Moving towards Brussels one day, a minor dogfight made an exciting spectacle almost immediately over our heads. A single seater fighter aircraft carrying RAF markings had just been down at low level, strafing, when two Luftwaffe fighters attacked it. The RAF machine got in a burst at one of the Germans and scored a hit causing the plane to disappear behind trees. The second German closed on the RAF machine and fired a prolonged burst at it. Smoke appeared and the airscrew stopped. The RAF machine dived at speed, levelled out as it got close to the ground and disappeared in an avenue between trees. In the excitement our Jeep left the road and ended up in a ditch. Some digging and levelling and the four-wheel drive eventually enabled us to get back on to the road.

We were none the worse for the crash, but sorting ourselves out took at least half an hour. We then drove down the avenue between the trees and we had only gone four hundred yards when we came across the pilot of the crashed RAF fighter, a Canadian, lying on the ground calmly smoking

No6 RAF Security Section pose for the camera next to their jeep, somewhere in Belgium.

NOBODY'S HERO

a cigarette. He appeared to be unhurt, but this turned out not to be the case. He said his leg was hurting him and when we came to have a look at it, we found that one of his legs was broken at the shin. There was some bleeding, which we staunched with a field dressing. We then collected a couple of spars of wood from a nearby gamekeeper's hide and fashioned a couple of crude splints which we affixed to the leg with the belt from his trousers, a bandage and tape from the first aid kit we carried on the Jeep. We then transported him to an RAF Unit, some distance away. His composure throughout was remarkable, but we supposed his good fortune at not being killed during the dogfight and being able to crash land safely in wooded terrain had something to do with his attitude.

An even more remarkable aspect was that he had succeeded in dragging himself at least half a mile from the spot where his plane had crash-landed. This with a broken leg, across uneven, untrodden ground, was no mean achievement.

THE LIBERATION OF BRUSSELS

Brussels, the capital of Belgium, was liberated on 3rd September, 1944. The Welsh Guards were the first to enter the City, but most of the German forces had left without putting up much of a fight. There were some minor pockets of resistance still to be eliminated, but we were able to move around the City without taking too many risks. For a short time there were reports of snipers operating from the bell tower of the famous Cathedrale St Guidule, but we neither saw nor heard proof of this.

We took some rooms for use as a base and office and we were inundated with problems from day one. We operated day and night to cope and there was no shortage of information about the things that had gone on during the German occupation.

Liberation of the whole of Belgium had been completely achieved and as was only to be expected in a city of the size and importance of Brussels, there were all kinds of forces at work, seeking to develop to their own narrow advantage the state of flux that existed now that the Germans had been ousted. Politically, there was a battle for power taking place from the first day. The Police service was in turmoil and we found ourselves trying to sort out who was legitimately in charge of what. We visited two particular Police Units both of which appeared to be seeking to establish themselves as being responsible for the policing of Brussels. People were being arrested and sidelined right, left and centre, some were imprisoned and, on a more sinister note, there were frequent reports of individuals being summarily tried and shot. People were certainly disappearing without trace.

We interrogated a number of collaborators and handed them over to the Belgian authorities. One Belgian citizen in particular, tried to slip through the net by a fairly ingenious ploy. He had been a minor trader in scrap metals when the occupation of Belgium by the Germans began, but by collaborating actively with the Germans, he made a lot of money. He became a well known collaborator and when it became obvious that the Germans were going to be driven out, he made contact with a family who had been hiding an RAF man who had parachuted to safety near Brussels after his plane had been damaged. The scrap man paid the family a large sum of money, through an intermediary, and took over the RAF airman's concealment without disclosing his own identity. When the Allies arrived in the area the scrap man came forward using the concealment of the RAF man as proof of his loyalty to the Allied cause. The matter then took an even more bizarre turn when the same scrap man was invited to be a guest at a Ball being arranged by the Allied Forces in Brussels, to celebrate the liberation of the City. Fortunately for those involved, one of our newly acquired female informants in the city came forward and denounced the scrap man for what he really was. We, as a Section, took appropriate action and the scrap man's past lead to his being arrested, almost on the eve of the Liberation Ball. The panic in certain high military quarters had to be seen to be believed, but justice had been done, and my Section had played a part in it.

The female informant mentioned was the 'Madame' of one of the upmarket brothels in the City, and what she did not know about the German hierarchy, and some of the Belgians, was scarcely worth knowing.

We spent time listening to her and she was truly a mine of reliable information. In the interests of discretion I shall call her 'Mimi'.

'Mimi' disliked the Germans so she used all the tricks of her trade to obtain information that might be of value to the Resistance movement. Her attitude to her method of gathering information from her German customers was quite whimsical and on numerous occasions she referred to the pillow as being equal to the confessional as a means of obtaining classified information!

She had a liking for Players cigarettes, which we were able to supply liberally in return for her information.

Sad to relate, Mimi may, in the end, have paid a dear price for providing information. She had a younger sister who had been privately educated at Mimi's expense and kept well away from the profession from which Mimi derived her income. Together with a colleague, I met the sister for a meal one evening and she was a really shy, demure young woman. Mimi kept a close watch on her, but one evening she failed to return home. Mimi sensed that something untoward had happened to her so she appealed to us for help. Out of deference to Mimi's wishes we scoured Brussels for days, but the young lady was still missing when we left Brussels in support of the Army's drive towards Holland. Our conclusion was that someone had settled a score with Mimi by having her sister 'bumped off'.

We had stayed in Brussels for three weeks. Antwerp was liberated on September 4th, 1944. The first British units reached the Dutch border on 13th September 1944. The town of Eindhoven was just fifteen miles away. Troops surprised the German bridge Guards at De Groot and they abandoned resistance. The advance into Holland proper had begun.

A typical German machine gun unit.

Dutch women accused of fraternising with the enemy during the years of occupation have their heads shaved as a punishment. Note the tufts of hair lying on the ground.

NOBODY'S HERO

CHAPTER TWELVE

The Liberation of Holland

As the Allied armies continued their progress towards the frontiers of Germany, the enemy's resistance stiffened. Patriotism was very much to the fore and the defenders realised that Holland was one of the gateways to their beloved Fatherland. They fought back with frantic bravery.

In support of the land war being fought in Holland, a massive airborne operation, Code-named 'Market Garden' was launched from bases in the United Kingdom. It began on 17th September, 1944 and ended in heroic failure on the 25th September, 1944.

The Allied troops who took part were the 1st British Airborne Division, two United States Airborne Divisions and the Polish Parachute Brigade. The Airborne drop was made on territory in the general area of the river Rhine and the mainland frontier with Germany. The main targets were key bridges across the lower Rhine, (called the Waal in Holland) at Nijmegen and the Rhine at Arnhem. The operation was launched from eight British and fourteen American airfields. Five hundred Gliders and their towing planes took part supported by a thousand British and American fighter aircraft.

Strong German army forces were located near the dropping zone and fierce fighting went on for days. Unfortunately the bulk of the Allied troops were landed too far away, their signalling equipment was found to be inadequate, their maps were not up to date and bad flying conditions prevented reinforcements from being provided in time.

A German General said of the Operation, "Almost before the British had touched the ground we were ready to defeat them."

The US/British Airborne assault was intended to:

(i)   seize bridges across rivers and canals in Holland;

(ii) outflank the German Siegfried Line defences;

(iii) clear the way for a rapid advance for the Allied Forces advancing through Holland.

If successful, the plan would have cut-off all German troops in the West of Holland and provided access to the port of Antwerp, thereby strengthening Allied supply lines. The assault was also intended to cut-off German rocket bases at The Hague.

But the plan ended in failure. The Allies lost over a thousand men and the Germans three thousand dead or wounded after an epic struggle. The defeat resulted in the failure of British and American forces to enter the German mainland in the year 1944. The rocket bases continued to deliver V1 and V2 rockets to their targets in London and Antwerp with resultant physical and psychological damage. Operation 'Market Garden' was perhaps the boldest Allied failure of World War 2. It might easily have shortened the war, but instead it turned out to be tragic failure.

Controversy raged for years afterwards as to whether a Dutchman, Christian Lindemanne, had leaked details of the Airborne assault to the Germans. War historians have since said that it was a mistake to launch Operation 'Market Garden' before the port of Antwerp was open for shipping. If logistical support for the Arnhem campaign had been easier and on a larger scale, the outcome might well have been different.

The first major ship was unloaded at the port of Antwerp on November 28th, two weeks after the Arnhem debacle and more than five months after the Normandy Landings.

An additional adverse factor was that the British Army's advance through Belgium and Holland had made insufficient progress to enable it to link-up with the Airborne troops fighting the Arnhem battle. The German armies had fought and lost in Normandy, France and Belgium, but Hitler had built up a new Army Group with which he launched a massive counteroffensive in the Ardennes, Belgium. What was more, this new force was intended not merely to hold the front, but to hurl itself against the weakest American sector, sweep westwards and reach the English Channel. What followed became known as 'The Battle of the Bulge'.

The onslaught was the heaviest Panzer tank attack ever seen on the Western Front and this necessitated the redeployment of Allied Forces that would otherwise have been able to advance through Holland and join up with the airborne forces at Arnhem.

When the final surrender came at Arnhem, the gap between the two forces was only a matter of a few miles, but this proved more than critical as far as the overall campaign to defeat the Germans was concerned.

The German counteroffensive was eventually halted, but it prevented the Allies entering the German mainland during the Autumn of 1944. The end result was that plans to move the attack into Germany had to be postponed.

At one stage my Section was in sight of the bridge at Nijmegen, but along with the remainder of the forces involved we were told that we would be spending the Winter of 1944 in Holland whilst the bulk of Dutch territory remained in German hands and this caused morale to drop substantially.

In September 1944 we moved into winter quarters in a school on the outskirts of the town of Eindhoven. The school was closed to its pupils, but we never did understand exactly why because we did not need the whole of the building for our purposes. But it may well have been the case that the displaced children were able to maintain their education at other schools, and perhaps mixing children with the military was unwise, anyway.

One extremely distressing aspect of our association with the school was that, knowing that the military were in residence, the pupils returned to the school and made a practice several times a day, of scavenging in our "pig bins" for food. They brought their paper bags with them and then made their way home with perhaps enough food to provide their families with a meal. There was a desperate shortage of food in the country at that time, so military units were visited regularly. As often as not we picked the children out in rotation and gave them sweets and chocolate to supplement their diet.

To add to everyone's misery the Germans were launching their V1 rocket weapon (the doodle bug) from launch sites not too far away. Some of the rockets were intended for the port of Antwerp, which the Allies were keen to bring into use so as to shorten their supply lines.

At least one rocket a day appeared overhead, flying erratically and out of control. One exploded about a quarter of a mile from my Section's billet and the building swayed from side to side to an alarming degree. The effect on our nervous systems was quite considerable, particularly as there were no air raid shelters. To add to the morale problem, the Luftwaffe made the occasional air raid on Eindhoven. There were precious few buildings with cellars and life, at times, became very trying.

One particularly vicious air raid took place about breakfast time on New Year's Day 1945 when the Luftwaffe attacked the local airfield. A number of Allied planes were destroyed on the ground, buildings were damaged and there were heavy casualties. The son of the then Canadian Prime Minister, Mackenzie-King was reported seriously wounded on the airfield.

Later the same day the Local Dutch Chief of Police contacted us and asked if we would visit his Headquarters where they were holding a German pilot who had been shot down and taken prisoner during the morning raid on Eindhoven airfield.

I proceeded to the Police station accompanied by a Dutch interpreter who spoke fluent German. We were taken to a cell-block and there, seated on a bench in a cell isolated from the rest, was a man in Luftwaffe uniform and flying boots. He was about twenty years of age, five feet nine inches tall, with blond hair and blue eyes; a typical Aryan. The Dutch police officer remained with us at my request.

The look of arrogance on the young man's face had to be seen to be believed and he refused to stand up. I eventually persuaded him to do so by taking my revolver out of its holster. My interpreter colleague proceeded to ask him the usual questions about his name, rank and number and to these he responded.

Further attempts to obtain information were ignored, but at each opportunity he led forth about the superiority of the German race, the German Air Force and their faith in the ultimate outcome of the war. He was certainly not afraid and we came away feeling that here was one young man whose faith in Hitler and the Nazi regime remained unshaken even though the Allies were poised close to the Rhine, waiting to complete the destruction of the German war machine. We later arranged his collection and transportation by the Army to a POW cage.

My Section settled down to an almost routine round of Security duties, but occasionally there were bizarre happenings. I had occasion to call on a Dutch family at home to interview one of the daughters who was engaged to a German airman who had been based at the local airfield. The association between the two proved to be of negligible security importance, so I left after about half an hour. As I moved away from the door of their home two shots rang out and I heard bullets splatter against the brick wall close to my head. I then heard someone running away, but I decided that as it was dark it was unwise to give chase. The people who had done the shooting remained unknown, but a clue as to their identity might have been provided a couple of days later when two male members of a Dutch resistance group calling themselves 'Blau Jagers' (blue hunters) called at the house probably with the intentions of shaving-off the young woman's hair (a practice often carried out on women who had associated with the German military). Fortunately, she was not at home, so the men left and did not return.

In a number of Dutch homes in the south of Holland at that time family life was very much under the influence of the Catholic Church and the longer we stayed there the more obvious this became. In Catholic homes in particular the standard of morality amongst the womenfolk was high. Something that struck me as being particularly odd was that mixed bathing was not permitted in the public swimming baths.

A minor upsurge in prostitution manifested itself and this produced a number of problems for the military. In one case in particular, we were eventually obliged to take action. Two sisters began charging for their services and quite a number of Servicemen became their customers. One of the sisters developed a minor VD infection, which was being passed on to servicemen. We were notified because RAF personnel were known to be visiting the place. I paid the girls' home a visit around mid-morning. Their usual 'hours' were from six in the evening. I knocked on the door and one of the two, wearing surprisingly little clothing answered and after a mild altercation agreed that I could have a look inside. The other sister was having her breakfast and at first she seemed to under the impression that my visit was taking place for other purposes.

I made them fully aware of the reason for my visit and proceeded to label the place as 'out of bounds'. I arranged for appropriate medical intervention and that particular problem subsided. I also visited the units whose men had been taking advantage of the facilities provided by the young ladies and remedial medical action was taken there.

Eindhoven is home to Philips, the giant Electrical manufacturers, and one of the most notable effects of having such a major employer in the town was that most of their many employees, in those days, went to work on bicycles. They rode to work in the morning rather spasmodically over a period of about half an hour, but at the end of the day they left the factory in a matter of minutes in solidly packed posses. The sight of them leaving the main gates *en masse* was almost unbelievable. Three or four abreast, handlebar to handlebar, nose to tail, they just took the roads over and it was pointless for anything to get in their way. Their exodus was beautifully organised and for a time parts of the town were entirely theirs. We became full of admiration for their cycling abilities, particularly as not one of the machines was fitted with the kind of calliper breaks found on British bicycles. Those skilful, intrepid riders relied on their back-pedalling brakes, but none of us ever saw a collision.

During the month of November 1944, I was granted leave to the UK from Holland. For me, this entailed a train journey from Eindhoven to the Hook of Holland, a North Sea crossing to Harwich, a train journey to London, and a further train journey to Nottingham.

Activity at the port of departure, the Hook of Holland, was interesting if only because there were some interesting looking packages and boxes being transported by Servicemen to the United Kingdom.

Obviously, troops had been given gifts as they moved along, and in Brussels, for instance, they had been able to buy presents for the family at home. One particular Airman stole the whole show. The train to the Hook was still standing in the station and this determined fellow was struggling to remove a huge wooden box from the Guard's Van. I estimated its size as being four feet by three by two. The carrying arrangement was two rope handles, one at each end. The box was more than the Airman could manage by himself, so I offered to help him carry it to the end of the platform leading to the gangplank of the boat that would be taking us to Harwich, England. It was certainly a heavy consignment.

As we staggered along the platform I could not help but read a notice the Airman had affixed to two sides of the box. On it was written the words, "Radiogram going home for repair".

The boat and train journeys were erratic and I just had to sit them out until I reached Victoria Station, Nottingham at around midnight the day after I had left my Unit.

My home was still twenty miles away, I was wearing a revolver and ammunition, and carrying a back pack and a small case. My mood was rock bottom, but I decided to walk the remaining twenty miles.

I had completed five miles and was beginning to regret that I had started the walk when a car pulled up. The driver, a man accompanied by his wife, offered me a lift to Mansfield, which would cut my walk journey by twelve miles. I was beginning to feel pleased and relieved, when the man asked where I had come from. I told him Holland. I then made the mistake of moaning about my rotten, tiring journey when the wife cut me off with the remark, "Our son was killed recently over Germany".

There was no further conversation between us and, in a sense, I was relieved when I alighted from the vehicle some twenty minutes later.

I finished the five miles stint that remained on foot, and arrived at my parents' house just as the coal miners were leaving their houses to start the day shift at the local colliery. House doors in mining villages were never locked, so I quietly let myself in, took off my revolver and pack and went to sleep on the rug in the parlour. It was about 6am. My parents woke me with a cup of tea some hours later.

After my return to Eindhoven, life for the Section took on a similar pattern to that which applied during our service in the United Kingdom, but there were some lighter moments.

One of our newly acquired Dutch interpreters had a friend who led a dance band which played music very much in the style of the celebrated Victor Sylvester dance orchestra. We arranged that they should play at a local restaurant, weekly, with a modest charge for admission. These occasions proved to be very popular, the band was earning money, the bar did a booming business and for a few hours life became very pleasant for some hundred or so servicemen and their locally acquired lady friends. I attended the dances with the eldest daughter of the family I had been visiting. One evening in particular, we were sitting in the bar at one of the dances when we were joined by an Army NCO and his lady friend and we spent a very pleasant evening together. I was intrigued by his accent so I began the process of finding out where his home was in England. After a few minutes I had established that this was in Nottingham. After a few more minutes I had established that he was, in fact, my cousin!

Philips were kind enough to put their magnificent Eindhoven theatre at the disposal of the Allied Forces. Entertainers were flown out regularly from England and some of the best West End shows came out lock, stock and barrel. Tommy Trinder, the comedian, brought the house down, but the two shows I remember best were the play *Yellow Sands* starring Emlyn Williams and a concert by the Joe Loss orchestra.

NOBODY'S HERO

The Philips factory also became important to my Section for another, but much less pleasant reason. For some years, the policy of the Nazi government had been to scoop up men from other European territories they had annexed and transfer them to France to work as slave labour on major construction projects, e.g. building military fortresses along the Channel coast. Thousands of men were taken away from their homes in this manner and they spent the occupation years boosting the work force of TODT, the infamous Nazi labour organisation.

The Baltic States, Poland and Czechoslovakia were among those countries whose citizens were rounded up for work in France and elsewhere and, as was only to be expected, they formed relationships, they fathered children and became family units in France and other occupied countries. The gradual collapse of the German military machine in France and Belgium meant that these displaced persons were able to consider their future as free citizens living, as aliens, in a foreign land. The pull of home was felt in some cases, but others would have been content to remain in France. In ordinary parlance they were an unspecified group of refugees. Matters for some of them took an unexpected turn for the worse when they were again rounded up by the French authorities whose intention it was to repatriate them to their countries of origin.

One such group was transported to Eindhoven during the winter of 1944. They were incarcerated in an empty building in a Philips factory enclave and we were charged with the task of ensuring that they did not abscond or cause too many problems.

The military provided sentries and our job was to deal with all the other matters that arose during the day. Beds were made available in barrack room fashion in an empty factory bay which had both cooking and washing facilities. The refugees in their respective family units were afforded little or no privacy and the problem this caused for us were limitless. One of the most unmanageable situations arose when couples started getting 'frisky' whilst children were running around.

The project lasted a matter of weeks and during this time we were able to glean some information as to their backgrounds and ethnic origins.

We talked about this and came to the conclusion that more than one ethnic group was present. They seemed to speak a patois of languages, but as a group they got on well together. We eventually formed the opinion that the bulk of them would have been happy to remain where they had been during the Occupation years.

On a given day their stay at the Philips factory came abruptly to an end. Army lorries arrived early one morning and before lunch time the "refugees" were embussed and driven away. We were not told of their destination, but one of the drivers let slip the fact that they were being taken to a port for shipment overseas. There was open speculation that this meant Russia. The operation was Code-named 'Black Tulip'. Many years later a major international controversy arose on the subject of Eastern Bloc subjects who were forcibly repatriated from Western Europe.

One of the unlikely developments arising from the static war situation was that, occasionally, the Germans made children part of the war game. In intelligence parlance these children became know as 'Line Crossers' and their activity was simplicity itself. Dutch families were keen to retain contact with friends and relatives on either side of the territory forming the war front and whilst roads bisecting the front lines were impassable it was possible for people to cross the line by using the many miles of waterways, fields and lanes which were also part of the front line. Once across individuals were free to roam more or less at will.

The Germans adopted the tactic of offering inducements, particularly food, for children to cross over and take note of markings on military vehicles on the Allied side. Each Battalion or Regiment had its mascot or regimental sign and these became a common sight as standard markings carried on vehicles. When the children returned to the German side, the gradual build-up of the kind of information they had obtained, enabled the Germans to determine which Allied units were present in given areas of the front. All the children had to do was to remember that all the lorries were carrying the sign of a Polar Bear or a Desert Rat or some such emblem. The Germans knew the markings and therefore knew which

Allied units were present in a given location. The weakness in the scheme was that the children were easily persuaded by the Allies to say what they were up to. A process of disinformation then became possible. Information gathering on a battlefield took various forms, but I never thought I would live to see the day when children took part.

Sporting events, with soccer proving the most popular, relieved the frustrations that developed during our stay in Eindhoven. Inter-unit matches took place and there was usually a worthwhile high tea to follow. In the school itself we had games such as table tennis and darts but cards was probably the most popular.

During off-duty periods we visited Dutch families and firm friendships developed. I visited one Dutch family once a week and took with me the day's rations I would have consumed had I eaten at the mess. There were four children, three girls and a boy and their mother. The father had died. They had little food day by day so they were hungry for most of the week. On the occasion of my weekly visit they ate better. My ration might have been part of a loaf, a tin of corned beef, some sugar, sardines, potatoes, fats, jam and vegetables. The family put these together with their own meagre rations and the mother worked miracles to produce a reasonable mid-day and evening meal. In return, they did my washing and ironing and the son brought me home a good class cigar every now and then. I helped keep them alive during the long, cold winter. One day a Doodle Bug that was off course landed a hundred yards from their home, so they were left with plyboard windows for several weeks.

One never to be forgotten, but rather macabre evening event arranged by the Town Major (a Major in the British Army with special liaison duties to perform with the Dutch) was a film shown in our School on the subject of sexually transmitted diseases. The place was packed and there must have been some two hundred servicemen sitting down. The film, which was American, went into a lot of detail and several men left the room feeling unwell. The film was intended as a shocker and it certainly succeeded. It lasted about three quarters of an hour and when the lights went up I had never seen shock so evident on so many men's faces.

Christmas came and went and there was a plentiful supply of leave passes to the UK. My Section had more or less exhausted its intended role as a Security unit and time dragged.

Rumours about an assault on the German mainland were plentiful throughout January and February, 1945, but by March it became obvious that the crossing of the Rhine was shortly to take place. The Army began to gear up and shortly before Easter there was a general movement of troops closer to the intended target, and my Section left its school winter home and moved near to the town of Venlo, close to the Rhine. Our enforced stay in Holland was almost over. The next big adventure was about to begin!

CHAPTER THIRTEEN

The Assault on Germany, 1945

At Easter, 1945 British Army Engineers succeeded in the immense task of fording the River Rhine with one of their legendary 'Bailey bridges' mounted on a series of pontoons; the chosen spot was at Wesel am Rhine. The British Engineers built their bridge right under the noses of the German Army. They sustained casualties, but their achievement was one of the outstanding engineering feats of the whole European campaign. The river at this point was wide and fast flowing and the Germans were able to increase the river's flow by controlling several man-made dams. The speed with which the bridge was built contributed enormously to the quick establishment of a firm Allied bridgehead on the east bank of the Rhine.

Lower down the Rhine at Remagen, the Americans, after a fierce battle, succeeded in taking another bridge and this proved to be a vital success. They took full advantage of their achievement and began to fan out into the German mainland. With British and Canadian armies poised for a drive across the Hanoverian plain the final battle for Germany was then in full swing.

Movement across the Bailey bridge at Wesel was continuous and heavy twenty-four hours a day and it was superbly handled by the Army's Corps of Military Police. Keeping the traffic flowing smoothly for days on end was a major achievement. Vehicles that broke down on the bridge were unceremoniously tipped over the parapet into the river (minus their occupants, naturally!).

My Section crossed the Rhine by the Bailey bridge on Good Friday. That same day Winston Churchill made his crossing by LCM (a motorised form of boat cum landing craft), his famous Homburg hat clearly in view. The Prime Minister's presence at the front was a tremendous boost for morale.

We were the first RAF unit to make the East Bank of the Rhine and this gave the Section a lot of satisfaction coming as it did on top of our having been first into Normandy, first into Belgium and first into Holland – a unique quartet of achievements which we had every reason to be proud of, particularly as our classification as a unit was 'non-combatant'.

On reaching the east bank of the river, a temporary dirt road provided us with access to a tarmac-covered road that fed into the main road system of the town of Wesel.

After crossing the bridge, we were held up in convoy for a short time and our stop was highlighted when the Army Commander, General Montgomery, swept by, flanked by his customary Military Police escort.

Legend had it that anyone who failed to salute the Great Man was charged with insubordination – but like so many wartime legends this

British troops advance through Wesel, surrounded by scenes of almost total destruction.

NOBODY'S HERO

may not have been based on fact. I played safe, however, by giving him the salute of a lifetime!

We motored on into the town of Wesel which had been heavily damaged during the assault. Eventually we found an empty yard at the rear of a disused office block and decided to make that our base for the rest of the day. There were precious few signs of life in the town and it became evident that the bulk of the population had either fled or was in hiding.

In tandem with the Army's overland assault, a massive Airborne Division drop (Operation 'Varsity') beyond the town was a total success and a firm bridgehead on the East bank of the Rhine was established, literally within hours.

Over a thousand Gliders and planes took part in Operation Varsity, protected by a force of nine hundred planes. This in itself was a sight never likely to be repeated. Many casualties were sustained on both sides. Dropping out of the sky onto a defended position was a very hazardous business for Allied paratroops.

The earlier Battle of the Bulge at Ardennes, Belgium had meant that the Allies were forced to make major adjustments to their battle plans before beginning the assault on the Rhine, but once under way their success was assured.

Fighting for the first time on German soil, every mile of ground was contested by the Germans with desperate tenacity, particularly in the British sector opposite the vast industrial belt known as The Ruhr.

In the towns it was house-to-house combat and the grim results of this were everywhere to be seen.

When victory finally came and the Allies had broken out into the German hinterland, the price that had been paid in casualties was high. The 21st Army Group sustained 22,000 casualties, of whom ten thousand were British, seven thousand American and five thousand Canadian.

This battle on the Rhine marked the last great fight between the Allies and the Germans. The Germans had been outdone in numbers, but not in tenacity and desperate courage. The Rhine crossing was said to be the largest assault river crossing of all time. The operation involved some one million, two hundred and fifty thousand men under General Montgomery's control. The assault zone had a frontage of just over twenty miles. There were German defences in some depth, and their troops fought like madmen. On March 28th, General Montgomery was able to announce that the battle of the Rhine had been won.

The heavy movement of men, equipment and vehicles across the Rhine and the battle itself made the discharge of our normal security duties very hazardous and an initial reconnaissance patrol by a party of three of our Dutch (German speaking) interpreters ended in stark tragedy. An enemy plane, the Messerschmidt ME-262, the very first jet fighter/bomber to be used by the Luftwaffe, dropped anti-personnel bombs in the street where the three were walking. All three were hit before they could take cover. Their injuries were substantial and even though they were transported to a nearby American field hospital with all possible speed, they died from their wounds. The effect of this on the Section was devastating. During the course of the next few days it was established that the three who had died were the first Dutch nationals to lose their lives during the campaign on German soil, and this being so, the Dutch and British Governments ordered that their bodies be returned to Holland to be buried with full military honours. I was instructed to arrange the return of the bodies to Eindhoven and I decided to undertake the task, personally.

This turned out to be a truly traumatic experience. On a given day, together with a colleague, I collected the bodies from the field hospital and we had the thankless task of trussing them up in blanket-type body bags provided by the hospital. We loaded the bodies into the rear of the truck and set-off on the return journey to Holland.

Our route took us back across the Rhine bridge – destination Eindhoven. Shortly after crossing the bridge, we came across a British soldier from one of the Highland Regiments, dressed in a kilt, carrying a

---

Author's Note: One could not fail to be impressed by the arrangements at the American Field hospital. Apart from the fact that it was all under canvas and had been brought into use in a matter of hours, the atmosphere was not unlike that which prevailed in the average hospital in England. The American doctors, male and female, and their nursing staff and orderlies were a credit to themselves and their country. They were obviously doing a magnificent job under extremely hazardous conditions.

NOBODY'S HERO

suitcase, and thumbing a lift. It was obvious he was going on leave and as he was on an open country road with all the traffic moving in the opposite direction we pulled up alongside him. He confirmed that he was going on leave and was trying to make Eindhoven his next stop. We explained that the only lift we could offer him was in the back, but he hesitated when we told him what we were carrying. He seemed to disbelieve us so he poked his head through the canvas and had a look for himself. He was obviously shaken to the core and made off down the road shaking his head and probably cursing his luck.

The journey itself was fairly uneventful and we eventually came to a halt in a side street in Eindhoven, mid-morning. We had considered contacting a Priest, or the Police to seek their help, but we were undecided and almost frightened as to what we should do for the best. We were still discussing what to do when the door of a Convent just across the street opened and out stepped two young Nuns dressed in black habits.

My colleague looked quizzically at me. He noted the curious look on my face and said, "They could be the answer to our problem." He climbed out of the cab and beckoned to the nuns, who waited for him to cross to their side of the street. I followed and after the briefest of introductions we explained to them why we were back in Eindhoven. Fortunately for us, one of the Nuns spoke reasonable English and communication with her was fairly easy. They had a brief conversation between themselves in their own language and then asked us to wait while they went back indoors. They returned after a short interval and explained that they would take the bodies over and prepare them for presentation to their families. I readily agreed because the damaged corpses were obviously in need of attention. We carried the bodies into the Convent and laid them on benches in a chapel.

The Mother Superior made telephone calls and our job was more or less done. We returned later in the day and our three deceased colleagues were dressed in white robes and their wounds skilfully concealed. White flowers had been placed between their toes. The transformation was almost unbelievable. We took our leave of the Nuns and made the return journey to our Unit at Wesel. We were later advised that our Dutch colleagues had been buried with full military honours.

Talking to my colleague some time afterwards he asked me if I thought the sudden appearance of the two Nuns had been an act of Divine Providence? I said that at the time I thought it was. Coincidences like that are hard to believe.

As the Army moved on we settled into a routine of sorting out Nazi officials in the towns and villages that fell in our path. At one stage, whilst moving about in German territory, we took to wearing flying overalls and these proved to be ideal wear for our field operations. As we travelled we found that wearing flying overalls was a sensible, positive means of conveying our RAF identity to others, particularly when away from our vehicles. This was important in the battle zone where the self-preservation order of the day usually was, "When in doubt, shoot first and ask questions afterwards". As things worked out, we did not have a lot of face-to-face contact with RAF units or personnel, the reason for this being that we kept close to a moving front whilst the RAF was operating from airfields at some distance in the rear. Part of the philosophy behind all this was that the Army Commander felt it was important to have a Royal Air Force presence on as wide a scale as was reasonable and as near the action as possible. We saw the wisdom of this on numerous occasions when we caught up with the infantry and armoured units. The thumbs-up sign was common and one particular occasion we were greeted with cheers by an Army patrol, probably in recognition of the valuable support being given to forward troops by RAF fighter and fighter-bomber squadrons.

The Army continued its advance across the Hanoverian plain and we, as a Section, followed closely behind. En route we paid brief visits to the important towns of Minden, Osnabruck and Hanover. The latter two had been very badly damaged by a mixture of air bombing and artillery shelling. There were precious few signs of life.

The Germans were still putting up resistance in spasms but its impact was diminishing, doubtless due to the heavy troop losses they were sustaining in France, Belgium and on the Russian front. Added to this was the fact that, by this time, they knew they were going to be defeated.

The pace of the advance was such that we were scarcely in one location for more than two or three days, but even so there were some interesting developments that kept us busy.

Two of our Dutch interpreters were out on patrol one day when one of their newly-made contacts persuaded them to interview a German lady who said she had a story that she thought might be of interest to the Allies. According to the lady, her husband had been closely involved with Hitler in the years before he became Chancellor and the two had become friends. When the lady's father-in-law realised what was happening, he began openly criticising the association his son was having with Hitler. The situation between father and son gradually became acrimonious and eventually the father started writing abusive letters to Hitler criticising the Nazi movement. Hitler resented this correspondence and told the son to tell the father to shut up. The son was unable to do this, and shortly afterwards the son met his death in suspicious circumstances. The correspondence between the father and Herr Hitler ceased – the problem had been solved in a bizarre manner. The information had no direct security value, but I noted it in my Report.

Moving about in the war zone was becoming slightly easier, but casualties continued to occur. One incident involving two of our colleagues ended in tragedy. We had on occasion throughout the campaign worked alongside another RAF Security Section and it was they who lost a colleague due to offensive action by a German farmer. The NCO in question was on patrol with a colleague, on motorbikes. They were intending to make certain enquiries at a farm run by a local Nazi, but as they approached the front of the farmhouse, shots rang out. Both men were hit and one of them was seriously wounded. The one who was less seriously wounded succeeded in dragging his colleague away from the line of fire and laid him down in the shelter of a brick wall. He rendered what first aid he could and then drove off to seek assistance. During his absence, his colleague died from loss of blood. He himself was treated for gunshot wounds. When news of the incident reached us at our base we decided to return as a party to the farm to sort things out. We gained access to the farmhouse without further casualties. We ascertained that the farmer, who turned out to be a First World War infantryman, as well as a Nazi, had fired the shots at our two colleagues. We took him into custody to await trial as a War criminal. As we were about to leave the farm a British tank arrived on the scene. I spoke to the Officer in charge and he decided to take some action. He brought his tank into the forecourt of the farm and fired several shells into the farmhouse itself. The tank then drove off. We left the area and returned to our base, sadder and wiser men. Our colleague was buried nearby. He was in his early twenties. Our other colleague recovered from his wounds and continued in service.

A patrol we made in the neighbourhood of the town of Minden was held up one morning when rifle and machine gun fire began to come at us from a small copse on one side of the road. The main Army thrust had gone through, so this was obviously a pocket of German troops whose job it was to harass those Allied troops who followed behind. We took cover and were considering retreating on to another route when a British armoured corps flame-throwing tank came on to the scene. There were further shots from the copse, so the flame-thrower Commander decided to take action. The tank moved slowly forward pouring out flame and the response was unbelievable. Within seconds there were terrifying screams from the copse and in a matter of minutes the action was over. We drove to our destination, unmolested. My flesh was still creeping hours later.

As was only to be expected contact with our base HQ was both remote and intermittent and this caused us the occasional supply problems, particularly as regards food. Petrol we could get from the Army, with little or no difficulty. At some intervals we were obliged to live almost off the countryside and this was not particularly difficult even when we entered the German mainland. On one particular day we were out as a party in Jeeps, with no forward rations. We had spent the previous night in a hedgerow and our breakfast of stale bread and a limited ration of bully beef left us feeling hungry. We made several house searches in the neighbourhood of the town of Minden and our last port of call was a farm where a particularly prominent local Nazi was thought to be in hiding.

At about lunch-time we drove up to the farm along an approach road about a quarter of a mile long and as we entered the farmyard we saw five young women run into a barn and secure the door behind them. A massively built man then appeared from the farmhouse and made his way towards us. He was obviously the farmer, so we explained that we would be searching the place. We could not fail to notice that he was sporting a magnificent gold watch chain, one part of which disappeared into the right hand pocket and the corresponding half into the left hand pocket of his waistcoat, clearly indicating the presence of two pocket watches.

We carried out our search, but did not find the man we were looking for. The farmer who came across as a fairly straightforward character denied all knowledge of the man and we were inclined to accept his word. Then, somewhat to our surprise, he asked if we would like some beer and we said we would. We trooped into the farmhouse where his wife was busy cooking what we assumed was the family's mid-day meal on a huge solid fuel stove on which stood several large cooking pots. As part of her preparations she lowered a rack, which had been out of sight up a large chimney, and selected a variety of sausages from a display that would not have disgraced a butchers' shop window!

The farmer returned to the kitchen accompanied by his five daughters, whose ages ranged from fifteen to twenty-five. They were a bit giggly, but they had the effect of thawing-out the atmosphere whilst we drank the beer. A few minutes later food was placed on a huge wooden table and we were invited to partake. This we did without a lot of hesitation and it was a good meal of potatoes, sauerkraut and sausage followed by tart, stewed apples and a drink that might possibly have been tea. It was interesting for us to note that by this time the farmer was no longer wearing his gold chain and watches.

We eventually left the farm after offering to pay something for the meal, but they would not hear of it. We could not help but feel that the five girls had found it all very exciting. The parents probably heaved a sigh of relief.

We moved on and we had not driven more than ten kilometres when one of my colleagues asked if we could stop, as he felt ill. We pulled off the road and in seconds he was doubled up with stomach pains. We had no means of medicating him, but he vomited and the pains soon subsided. Having been warned not to drink German water or eat their food, the thought flashed through my mind that the farmer might have poisoned us, and for at least the rest of that day we all felt a bit queasy.

I even went to the trouble of looking at my tongue in the mirror and it certainly looked black. I mentioned this some time later to a Medical Officer and he said it was probably the effects of the acid in the stewed apples combined with the mysterious drink we thought might have been tea. Needless to say, we did no more eating out. The knock-on effect on one man having a stomach upset was interesting, if only because it served to demonstrate what can happen elsewhere in the body when the mind starts to work overtime.

From time to time, one of the means we adopted for relieving tension was to drink alcohol in short, sharp, but effective doses. For a few hours thereafter the world appeared to be a different place and we all felt better for having relaxed. One attempt to create a cocktail based on vehicle radiator anti-freeze proved to be quite an adventurous project, but the end result did not justify the effort. All we got was an uncomfortable feeling in the pit of the stomach. Soon afterwards, however, a resourceful colleague came across a quantity of bottles of brandy in the basement of a bombed-out, derelict building, and this helped considerably. It was Hennessy Four Star.

For about a week or so thereafter we had brandy for breakfast, brandy for lunch and brandy for tea, and were none the worse for the experience. At the entrance to the next village we came to, we were interested to note a sign prominently displayed which said, "Looters will be shot". With the pleasant effects of the brandy still in our systems, the sign had the salutary effect of reminding us that we were members of the Police Branch of the Royal Air Force.

One important town taken in the Army's continuing drive eastwards was that of Celle which lay between Hanover and Luneberg.

We reached the town centre shortly after effective German resistance had ceased and the remnants of their battered garrison were fleeing eastwards. Occasional bursts of small arms fire were heard and the odd explosion, but in substance, the town had been captured.

We began to search for a building in which to establish an operating base, but this proved difficult because the bombardment had caused extensive damage to property. Very few buildings remained intact and there was an eerie gloom about the whole place. We eventually came across a Doctor's house that had survived the shelling. The Doctor and his wife were still in residence and after a short discussion with them we requisitioned the premises for use as an office. We allowed the doctor to retain the upper floors as a surgery and living quarters. There was no friction between us, and the arrangement proved to be a success from both points of view. An outbuilding afforded us additional accommodation.

The Doctor's main downstairs room provided a desk and a telephone which was still connected. Considering the damage to the town's telephone installations and lines, this was little short of a miracle. We displayed an official RAF notice at the front of the house stating who and what we were. It appeared likely that we would remain in the town for some time.

After a brief period of settling-in and cleaning weapons and uniforms, our days were spent seeking out prominent Nazis and taking them into custody, the Army providing the necessary custodial arrangements in a local gaol. We also dealt with hordes of prisoners of war who were being shepherded away from the front line. At times they were so great in

---

Author's Note: Nebelwerfers were multi-barrelled mortar projectors whose bombs were fitted with a siren which caused them to wail as they flew through the air. They were nicknamed "Moaning Minnies". The Germans had developed the use of mortars to a high degree of effectiveness and they took a heavy toll on the Allied Forces. Another type of mortar fired "stonks" which landed without warning, grating the nerves of those at the receiving end. Thirty-five pound missiles could be thrown a distance of three miles by these weapons.

number that there were insufficient POW cages available to take them, so the Army provided a Jeep front and back of the columns and the odd armed soldier walking along the flanks. We estimated that the largest column was a thousand strong and they were given the strict instruction to keep on walking. This they did and our last sight of them was their tail end disappearing down the road more or less due west.

On one particular morning, I was sitting at the desk, when to my surprise the telephone rang. I answered in English and a female voice at the other end asked if I was the person in charge. Her command of the English language was good, but I assumed she was German. I hesitated for some seconds then asked her to say what it was that she wanted. She replied to the effect that her husband was a senior German Army Officer who wished to surrender to the British. I asked the woman where her husband could be found and she explained that he was with her at their home in another part of the town. I asked her to hold the line and spent the next few seconds wondering whether the whole thing may be some kind of hoax or a trap. Some team members were still at hand, so I picked up the telephone, took down the address and told her that we would call on them shortly.

Four of us piled into a Jeep, with weapons, and off we drove. Having acquired a town map from the Doctor we soon arrived at the address, an imposing looking detached house, only slightly damaged. I posted one man at the back of the house and one at each of the two sides. I was half expecting that something unusual would happen so I loosened the flap on my revolver holster and proceeded to knock on the front door. A woman answered and invited me to step inside. She was a tall, elegant person probably in her early fifties, smartly dressed and possessed of a very attractive head of hair. It occurred to me afterwards that she had probably gone to considerable pains to prepare herself for the occasion. She said her husband was ready and waiting for our visit. She preceded me down the corridor and indicated a door on the right that she explained was her husband's study.

I knocked and entered and there, sitting in a large armchair, was a German Army General in full ceremonial dress, his head held high, at an angle, and his right hand on his sword, which was resting on the floor. His portrait in oils was on the wall immediately behind him. A truly mind boggling scene. Not being sure what to do for the best I saluted and told him that I would comply with his request and deliver him to a POW Camp which had been established just outside the town. He explained that he had been responsible for Nebelwerfers,* but his Division had been over-run. He put on his Greatcoat and cap and followed me to the Jeep. I asked him to take the front seat alongside the driver and this he proceeded to do. I climbed into the back with the other members of the team, one of whom was clumsy in putting his Sten gun down on the Jeep floor to the extent that it fired a bullet. The missile passed between the General and the driver and fortunately no harm was done.

The General did not turn a hair, but I very nearly had a convulsion. The thought of taking a General prisoner and then shooting him from behind was almost too much to bear. Needless to say the NCO responsible got the whip end of my tongue when we returned to base. The General was safely handed over to the Officer in Charge of the Prisoner of War cage and I was inwardly delighted at the thought that I was probably the only member of the Royal Air Force to take a German Army General prisoner, on a one-to-one basis, during the whole of the 1939-45 war. As far as I know, this is a fact.

The infamous Concentration Camp at Belsen was just a few miles up the road and one day we were made aware of this when an unexpected male visitor walked into our office. To describe his movement as walking is perhaps misleading for he was bent almost double and shuffled one foot in front of the other to achieve forward momentum. His head was shaven and he looked like a skeleton wearing a shirt, trousers and shoes. He spoke no English and it was difficult to make out what he was saying even in German, his native tongue. It was pointless to ask him to sit down because the shape of his body made this an impossibility. It dawned on us fairly quickly that he had "walked" the distance from Belsen to Celle in order to establish his freedom from imprisonment at the Concentration Camp. We tried plying him with food and drink with only very limited success. It soon became evident to us that there was nothing we could do to help him so we conveyed him to a nearby German civilian hospital that was actively tending both military and civilian casualties. We handed him over to the Doctor in charge with instructions that he was to be given proper care and treatment. We satisfied ourselves that he was in good hands.

We visited the hospital for a number of days afterwards and we were pleased to note that his physical and mental condition appeared to be improving. Our involvement with him was outside our normal terms of reference but simple, humanitarian considerations dictated that we gave him some help. We made several attempts to guess his age and our nearest guess was fifteen years adrift. He turned out to be not more than forty years of age. He was a survivor of the holocaust, but only just. We were content that we had played a small part in his return to civilisation.

As our stay in Celle continued, we gradually began to believe that the end of the war was in sight; but regrettably our sensing victory induced in us a degree of over-confidence. This resulted in our becoming careless and casual, ignoring the 'rules' drummed into us on the survival training courses in the UK.

When vacating towns, the retreating German forces went to a lot of trouble to set 'booby-traps', particularly in and around buildings and these caused numerous casualties, some of them fatal. Part of our work required us to enter buildings and we were lucky not to have walked into a trap. One of our number did set a booby trap off one day, and it was only the fact that a thick wooden door was open at a particular angle that saved him from injury or worse. He kept quiet about his escape for weeks but he had been very close to death.

The fluid position of the battlefront also presented problems which put us under constant pressure when out in the open. The shooting war was still close at hand and as the main Army thrust went ahead there were inevitably pockets of resistance left behind. The mopping-up of these pockets did not always take place immediately, if at all, so journeys outside the town had to be undertaken very cautiously. Identifying who was who, was at times, almost impossible and we always had in mind the thought that even though the people on the move were refugees or prisoners, some of them could still be the enemy.

We sought, as best we could, to escape from the dangerous daily grind, and one of our evenings whilst still at the Doctor's house stands out in my memory. It took the form of a most enjoyable musical occasion that came about almost by accident. One of the members of an Army unit billeted quite close to our office was a pianist whose interests lay in classical music. His pre-war ambition had been to be a concert pianist. One day whilst I was chatting to the Doctor about something totally dissociated from the war, I happened to mention the man's interest in music. This led the Doctor to say that he had a piano in his upstairs flat and the soldier was free to use it, if he so wished.

That same evening we had two hours of Chopin, Haydn, Brahms and Beethoven. The circumstances were unreal, but there we were, a group of British Servicemen and two Germans, in an active war zone, enjoying a musical soirée. The atmosphere was pure magic and for all present the war ceased to exist for a few precious moments.

When some days later we finally moved out of their house, most of us felt that the Doctor and his wife had become friends of ours. The order of the day for Allied troops was strict non-fraternisation, but what does one do in such circumstances?

Another happening of a lighter nature occurred as I left the office one morning and was about to climb into one of our Jeeps. An elderly lady, walking the footpath, dressed all in black and sporting a hat that would have not been out of place at Ascot Races called out to me in a cultured English voice, "Excuse me, young man, but are you here to stay?"

I would have guessed her age at not less than seventy. She chatted for something like five minutes during which time she explained that she had married a German subject prior to the war and Germany had therefore become her home. Her husband had died in the previous year. She mentioned that her movements had not been affected or interfered with in any way by the German authorities and she had retained her British nationality throughout. Our little *tête à tête* was quite a novelty, occurring as it did close to the shooting zone.

Probably the only really hilarious part of our days in Celle took the form of a pantomime provided one morning by a column of Italian servicemen, mainly soldiers, who streamed into the town to surrender to the British. They were accompanied by their wives, their girlfriends, their children and some of their belongings, but how they got together in Celle was a mystery we were never able to solve.

A full Army Colonel, dressed up like a dog's dinner, led the column. He walked immediately behind a huge Italian national flag mounted in a baby's perambulator (the baby was not in the pram!).

In total there must have been something like five to six hundred people in the column and nearly all the women were in tears. The sights and sounds on display were truly unbelievable, but in spite of all that was going on behind him, the Colonel held his head high, marched in a disciplined way, and obviously was doing his best for his country. The whole scene would not have been out of place at the La Scala opera house.

When he was level with our office, and having seen our sign hearing the RAF Roundel, the Colonel call his 'battalion' to a halt, came across and after saluting with great aplomb, said he wished to surrender his unit to the British. We gave him the same instructions we gave the rest of the prisoners – "Keep walking West" – and this they did.

By this time most of the women had stopped crying and some were even smiling. The children waved to us as though they sensed what nice, kind people the British were and it was noticeable that they seemed far less concerned about their predicament than their parents. But at least for them the war was over and possibly some of them were being reunited with their families for the first time in a long time. Strange as it may seem, they proved to be a light interlude in an otherwise drab existence.

Not everything that happened in the drive across Germany came to prominence, but one small incident did strike us at the time as being

No6 RAF Security Section and jeep, outside the Doctor's house, Celle, Germany. The author is at the wheel.

NOBODY'S HERO

important. At later stages of the advance, the RAF began to fly-in supplies using multi-engined aircraft. This, as we were to witness at first-hand, was a hazardous business, calling for airmanship of the highest quality. We were skirting a wood when a four-engined aircraft suddenly appeared a matter of feet above the trees at the wood's edge. It was flying so low that we all ducked as it passed overhead. The machine touched down and came to a halt in a field only a short distance from a ditch. We concluded that landing on that piece of ground had not been part of the crew's briefing in the United Kingdom. It was an exceptionally skilful piece of flying, made necessary, we assumed, by the need to maintain an adequate level of supplies in a very fluid combat situation. Four-engined RAF aircraft over the forward war zone in broad daylight were indeed a rare sight.

We did not remain in the area long enough to watch their take off, but doubtless it demanded an equally high level of risk and skill as had landing.

At this stage of the campaign there was the daily rumour that the war had ended and we all found this very frustrating. We happened to be approaching Luneberg (where the Peace Treaty was finally signed) and vehicles that passed us were giving out 'the war has ended' information as though it was authentic. After seven days of such rumours, we didn't even bother to listen.

We arrived at the town of Luneberg, requisitioned another house, and carried out an extensive round of duties in tandem with our colleagues from 84 Group, 2TAF. Their Section had been operating in parallel with ourselves from the Bridgehead onwards and inevitably our paths crossed.

Probably the most outstanding feature of this particular period was the increasing problem of prisoners of war and refugees fleeing from Eastern Germany in an attempt to avoid the advance of the Russian Red Army. One of the main roles we found ourselves playing was that of demonstrating a British Military presence, if only for a few days.

At one stage of our journey we had a break for a meal alongside a railway siding. There was little movement on the railway itself, due primarily to the constant raids on railway traffic by planes of the Royal Air Force. In one particular part of the siding, a column of a dozen or so railway carriages presented one of the most bizarre sights we witnessed throughout the whole campaign. Alongside each carriage in letters eighteen inches high were painted the words, *Nur Fuhr Schwer Kriegs Beschadigen*. Roughly translated this means 'only for severely wounded war casualties'. The words were joined together as one long word. German infantrymen occupied the carriages and Red Cross staff were carrying out a feeding operation from a field kitchen.

I walked the length of the train and the sights were unbelievable. In every compartment there were men without one or other of their limbs. In the worst cases both legs were missing. In some, the casualties were prone on the carriage floor and suffering from body wounds. German military and civilian medical personnel were dressing wounds and dispensing medication. I estimated that there were probably five hundred wounded men, all told.

I spoke to one of the Red Cross supervisors and she told me that the men had sustained their injuries during a major infantry battle with the Russian army during the German Army's retreat from the Eastern Front.

Our orders at this time were to continue moving north towards the Danish frontier, avoiding the City of Hamburg, which the Allied Air Forces had reduced to rubble. One woman interviewed by us later described the night of one of the 'thousand bomber raids' when Hamburg city centre had been heavily attacked. She explained that the atmosphere was so foul that hundreds of people had waded into the ornamental lakes that were a feature of the famous Alster area of the city centre and held their heads slightly above water level in order to be able to breathe. Buildings were on fire, there was heavy dust from the bombardment and their best chance of surviving was to remain thigh deep in water until the air raid had ceased. Hamburg was occupied by Allied troops on 3rd April, 1945.

The port of Lubeck on the Baltic Sea was an important strategic landmark and was soon in British hands. German resistance throughout the month of April 1945 became weaker and it was obvious with the Russians tearing into East Germany, that the end of the war was clearly in sight. This in itself produced pressures because we were all sensitive to the fact that, having survived the major crises of the campaign, it would be the worst possible outcome to be wounded or killed with the end in sight.

Our orders continued to be fluid and we were left to fend for ourselves. It was unlikely that a stay in the port of Lubeck would be of much importance, so we proceeded to move north into the Province of Schleswig-Holstein and in the direction of the German/Danish frontier. The city of Kiel was important because it had been the major base for the German U-Boat fleet and the Kriegsmarine (Germany's equivalent of the Royal Navy).

On 30th April, 1945, Adolf Hitler, German Chancellor and Fuhrer, committed suicide in a bunker at the rear of the Chancellery in Berlin. Grand Admiral Doenitz became his successor as Chancellor.

On the 3rd May, 1945, the Germans came to surrender at 21 Army Group Headquarters at Luneberg. They were sent away but returned on 5th May to hear and sign the terms of unconditional surrender, read to them by the Army Group Commander, General Montgomery.

By this time my unit was moving north towards the town of Schleswig. On the day following the surrender we had the hair-raising experience of being fired on by a German Armoured car from a distance of about four hundred yards. Fortunately no damage was done and we were able to accelerate out of danger. These were the very last shots we witnessed being fired in anger. This happened precisely one day after the war had officially ended and I have to admit to being shaken to the core.

Denmark and Norway had been under German occupation from April 1940; British Troops had finally liberated both countries in May 1945.

My Section moved as far north as the town of Schleswig and our journeying was almost at an end. We took up temporary residence in the town to await the arrival of other Sections and our base Headquarters unit.

CHAPTER FOURTEEN

Germany after the Surrender

My Section remained in Schleswig for a time and we were together with
our 84 Group colleagues and Headquarters Staff for a matter of days. A
period of debriefing and consolidation took place during the early part of
May 1945 and I received a further promotion to Flight Sergeant at this
time. My Section was then given responsibility for Security in the Kreis
of Sud-Tondern and almost immediately, we took up residence in the Kreis
capital town, Neibull (A Kreis is roughly the equivalent of a British
county).

Our principal tasks were to locate and arrest prominent Nazis; to vet
and appoint police officers and policemen; to trace and arrest war
criminals; to detect and suppress subversive movements; and generally to
check on morale and opinion amongst the population, particularly refugees
and prisoners of war. Our territorial responsibilities included the North
Sea coast islands of Sylt, Fohr, and Amrum and a non-public border
crossing into Denmark. The crossing was heavily fortified with barbed
wire and the troops manning the area were on orders to fire at intruders.

Our base was a large, comfortable detached house and we had our own
jail, nearby, manned by the British Army. Our prisoners, numbering ten
per week on average, were collected once a week and transported elsewhere
by the Army according to their type and category. Certain Nazi officials,
by rank, had been placed in an automatic arrest category, so their detection
and arrest was our main task. Interrogation was usually only a minor aspect
of their incarceration, as we soon acquired information that made their
attempts to conceal their past activities impossible.

We were particularly fortunate in this respect because, purely by chance, we came across the Party records intact in a local office. These records were personal files known as *Personalakten*; they included not only a photograph of the Nazi, but his complete Party history from the date he made his original application to join. These proved to be a real find, particularly when we had the individual with us face to face. In those instances where individuals were lying about their past, we were able to play cat and mouse with them, springing the trap at the last minute by handing them their file. We seldom had occasion to do this, but their reactions when we did so were scarcely describable. Some tried to maintain their innocence but most were soon brought down to earth with a bump. One interesting observation of our 'de-Nazifying' activities was that women were very seldom involved. The real activists were almost invariably men.

Another important duty involved regular liaison with the Town Major, a British officer who was the military boss of all he surveyed. Close contact with him was both necessary and fruitful. In a way he was kind of military equivalent to a modern day Town Mayor and he certainly had wide ranging powers. For one reason or another we had almost daily contact with him.

We gradually got to know almost every part of the Kreis and one of our special interest sites contained a ramp from which V Rockets had been fired. This proved to be an irresistible 'photo-opportunity' for British forces in the area, who took turns at sitting proudly on one of the rockets, still on the firing ramp, to have their pictures taken.

Perhaps our most important arrest around this time involved a senior Gestapo officer who had been in post in Copenhagen, Denmark, during the German occupation. He was in hiding on a remote farmstead just a few kilometres on our side of the German/Danish border. An informant provided us with information as to his whereabouts, so we carried out a dawn raid. We were six strong and well armed. We surrounded the site and I banged hard on the front door. We could hear scuffling inside, but no one came to the door. After a brief interval, I heard shouting at the back of the house and when I got round there our man could be seen trying to make a break for it, dressed only in his underwear. Rather to our surprise he seemed quite unperturbed when we took him back to base. We locked him in a room and left him to stew for the best part of the day. I then went in to speak to him and he almost immediately came out with the statement that he did not want to be interrogated. He asked that we provide him with paper and a typewriter and he would tell his story. I agreed to this and he was at the machine for nearly the whole day. We fed him at intervals and read his story as it came off the machine. Most of it was of little real interest, but one reference concerned the German Hierarchy and the flying of the Danish flag over the Royal residence in Copenhagen. He had received orders from the Reich Chancellery that the flag to be flown from official buildings in Copenhagen was to be the Nazi Swastika. Our man duly approached officials at the Royal residence, passed on the message from the Chancellery, but the answer that came back was a refusal. He notified Berlin who responded by ordering him to send troops in to remove the Danish flag and install the Nazi flag. The troops did the job, but by the time they were back in the street, the Danish flag was flying again, where it stayed throughout the German Occupation.

We kept him as our prisoner for a couple of days and he gave us a lot of food for thought as to how he came to have achieved a senior rank in the Gestapo. His explanation, which we eventually came to accept as reasonable and probably true, was that when the Nazis came to power in the early 1930s, he was a career policeman achieving regular promotion. The Nazis came to power in the putsch of 1933 and members of the Police service were gradually put under heavy pressure to become Nazi Party members. He joined, he said, because he knew he would get no further promotion if he didn't and he recognised that standing aside would have been seen as defiance. He gradually achieved senior rank in the police service and when the Germans annexed Denmark he was sent to Copenhagen because he was considered to be a moderate Nazi and the German Government were anxious to avoid a lot of friction with the people of Denmark. His plea to us, of course, was that he was not a dyed in the wool Gestapo man, but a victim of circumstances well outside his control.

The remainder of his "confession" was of little or no value to the British, but we were soon requested to provide members of the Danish Security Service with access to him. This we did and shortly afterwards he was closeted at our office with two Danish Security officers for the best part of a day. We received disposal instructions a day or so later and the last time we set eyes on him he was sitting in the back of an Army truck with an armed guard, awaiting shipment elsewhere. We assumed it was Denmark.

We spent the following weeks vetting the Police force and this proved to be a difficult task. We began the job by giving each individual a questionnaire known as a *Fragebogen*. This was a four-page foolscap document that asked a number of questions, each one of which the individual was obliged to answer. The first question was *Waren Sie jemals em mitglied der NSDAP?* (Were you ever a member of the National Socialist Workers Party?) Only one applicant in five replied 'yes'. We then proceeded to persuade them otherwise and they usually agreed. Some of those interviewed we rejected, some we approved for further service, some we arrested because their past histories were either suspect or already known to us. All in all, it was a big responsibility that we did not particularly like or welcome, but it was part of the job. The fear at the back of our minds was that we would let men who had been real Nazis slip through the net.

Our task in general was made even more difficult because the area was invaded by something like three thousand refugees/prisoners of war in the first few months of our stay. They turned out to be a motley bunch, as one might expect, and their ranks undoubtedly included wanted Nazis and war criminals who were keen to pose as refugees in the hope of escaping arrest. Others were senior Army officers trying to hide their Nazi past. Quite a number of them held out the forlorn hope that if they got close enough to the Danish border they might be able to slip across and escape detection altogether. The remainder were the flotsam of war who were only concerned about being in the British zone away from the

Russians. Food and accommodation were scarce and there was little work, so to us their presence was just another problem.

Without doubt the security highlight of our early days in Kreis Sud-Tondern arose from a tip-off given us by an Officer in the German police service. He came to our office early one morning and said he had some information he felt would be extremely interesting to the British. He directed me, together with three suitably armed colleagues, to a point very close to the Danish frontier, but still within the Kreis of Sud-Tondern. We alighted in open country and walked across a field to a place where he pointed to wheel tracks that he maintained had been made by an aeroplane landing and taking off during the previous night. We followed the tracks for three to four hundred yards, and close to a hedge they came to a stop. He drew my attention to some empty petrol cans and also to a cairn of stones that were still quite hot. The embers of a fire, which had been made inside the cairn, were hot and there were empty food tins and other items indicating that a meal had been taken there. He then pointed to the cairn and said, "Martin Bormann was here last night" (Bormann was Hitler's deputy). I questioned my informant further and he remained convinced that what he was telling me was the truth. Back at base, we discussed the matter for days and had to accept the fact that an aeroplane had landed in the field and whoever was in it must have been a VIP to justify being flown into the area. The other intriguing question, which haunted us for days, was: 'Was it really Martin Bormann, and if not, who was it'. The police officer remained adamant that the VIP had been Martin Bormann.

The proximity of the flight to the Danish border also provided interesting food for thought. When the plane took off again did it hop over the frontier wire and make a getaway? Some of the facts were indisputable. The police officer maintained that his tip-off came in by telephone from an anonymous source. He was totally convinced. I wanted to believe him, but it was such a long shot that in the end I convinced myself that it could not possibly have been Hitler's deputy.

Some years later, however, it was being freely reported that Martin Bormann had escaped via Denmark and was in hiding in South America. I got to thinking, on occasion, that had matters turned out differently I might have become famous. I was possibly present at the site of the last meal in Germany of the most wanted man in the world only 12 hours after his escape. Had I known of his whereabouts sooner I might well have had the opportunity to take him into custody.

During my post war work as an Intelligence Officer in Germany I had occasion to visit the cottage in Kupermuhle close to the Danish frontier where William Joyce (Lord Haw Haw) and his wife had been hiding at the time of his arrest. The purpose of my visit was to establish whether Mrs Joyce was still living at the cottage and to collect Joyce's personal effects and belongings. Joyce was later tried and hanged as a Traitor.

A number of bizarre coincidences had caused our paths to come close to crossing on previous occasions. Talking to my wife about Joyce some years later, I discovered that for a period of time, pre-war, he had lived next door to her family at an address in Earls Court, London. Also, on the night prior to our 1949 Civil Wedding at the British Consulate in Hamburg, my wife and I stayed at the Atlantic Hotel and we had our Wedding Breakfast the next day at the Vier Jahreszeiten (Four Seasons) Hotel. After fleeing from Berlin to Hamburg to avoid capture, William Joyce and his wife stayed at both these hotels whilst awaiting instructions from Berlin for William to continue his infamous 'Germany Calling' broadcasts from the "Reichsender Hamburg".

Joyce was probably the number one British traitor of the 1939-45 war and his activities in support of Hitler and Nazism were the subject of all kinds of speculation. Also, for some strange reason, there were conflicting statements made about his precise physical appearance. I am able to make a small contribution in this respect. When I visited the cottage at Kupfermuhle I took away, among other things, Joyce's one and only suit and I found it hard to believe that the trousers would have been big enough to fit a fully grown man, so I measured the inside leg. It was twenty-one inches, so from this one might reasonably assume that he was no more than about five feet two inches or five feet three inches tall.

From time to time information reached us concerning a Nazi organisation that had reputedly been formed when defeat for Germany seemed inevitable. This was said to be under the leadership of Otto Skorzeny and the organisation's recognition mark was the Edelweiss flower. Members, apparently, were encouraged to wear the flower in their lapels as a recognition mark. Initially, someone had the idea that Edelweiss members would keep alive the Nazi ideology and carry out acts of sabotage, but I personally only ever interviewed one German who said he knew of the organisation.

Otto Skorzeny was the man chosen by Hitler to rescue the Italian Dictator, Benito Mussolini from his captivity in the Abruzzi Mountains. When Mussolini fell from power, Marshal Budogho became head of the Italian State and his government had ordered Mussolini's arrest. Skorzeny was a Waffen SS Colonel who played a leading part in rounding-up those who had taken part in the plot to assassinate Hitler. Skorzeny also led a crack SS unit to arrest Admiral Horthy, a Nazi sympathiser, who was Head of State in Hungary. Skorzeny also directed the infiltration of hundreds of English-speaking Germans clad in American Army uniforms into the American ranks during the Battle of the Bulge in the Ardennes, Belgium. This was at the turn of the year 1944-45.

Skorzeny was acquitted at the 1947 Nurenberg trials of German War Criminals on the testimony of British Officers who gave evidence that he had done nothing his allied counterparts would not have done. Whilst awaiting a further trial as a leading Nazi in 1949 he escaped and spent his remaining years in Spain. He died there in July 1975 in Madrid.

Continuing our search and arrest activities, one particularly important local Nazi official proved difficult for us to contact, but it was reported time and again that he was in hiding in our locality. We had had several tip-offs, which led us to raiding no fewer than three houses, but we were unable to find him. He obviously lived under more than one roof but the fourth tip-off turned out to be more reliable. One night at about 11pm, together with two colleagues I went to a house, tried the doors and found that a door at the rear was unlocked. I posted one colleague at the side door and one at the front door. Through a chink in the curtains at the rear window, I could see that a man and a woman were in bed. I quietly let myself in, opened the bedroom door and switched on the light.

The man in the bed turned out to be the man we were hunting. What I had not expected to discover as I entered the room was that they were in the process physically demonstrating their affection for each other. After a few awkward moments I persuaded the man to get dressed and accompany me to our local detention unit. He turned out to be one of the top Nazi officials in the Kreis Sud Tondern hierarchy. I only caught a very brief glimpse of his female partner's face, before she dived under the sheets and stayed there.

Having the three islands to look after was a fairly pleasant part of the job. Sylt was a bathers' paradise reached at low tide across a causeway. Fohr and Amrum were not security hot beds, but we did take some people who were hiding there into custody.

A young woman who had been the local German Garrison Commander's secretary on the island of Sylt presented herself to us on one of our visits and offered her services. We did not take her on, but for some unexplained reason she continued to supply us with information. She stayed around for weeks hoping that we might change our minds but we didn't. She made great play of the fact she had a number of friends in England and visited them regularly before the war. She was a plausible individual, but there were aspects of her story that did not add up. In the circumstances it was not possible to check her account of her services with the German military and I held the personal view that someone had seen fit to send her to us for the purpose of penetrating our organisation.

The nearest town of any size was that of Flensburg, which, during the war, had received RAF Bomber Command's attention on more than one occasion. The international frontier crossing into Denmark came within its boundaries. The crossing point was known as Krusaa in German or Apenrade in Danish. It was a key area bearing in mind all the Nazis who were trying to use the crossing for escape purposes. Security in Kreis Flensburg was the separate responsibility of No 318 Army Intelligence Team.

We worked together with them as occasion demanded and monthly meetings became a feature of our lives. One of their Team members was a spectacular character of Mediterranean origin who could converse fluently in seven European languages. Our relationship with 318 was first-class.

In the period following the ceasefire, a state of 'non-fraternisation' existed, but this proved difficult to maintain. We had our own money printed in note form and designated 'British Armed Forces Special Vouchers'. The notes were denominated as sixpence, one shilling, five shillings and one pound and were valid only for transactions within 'official canteens and organisations'. We were not permitted to transfer them to any person not entitled to use British service canteens. Improper use of the notes rendered the offender liable to prosecution.

We were kept very busy throughout the remainder of 1945, but there was some time for relaxation as well. We played athletic games, we swam and we sun-bathed. The theatre at Flensburg put on first-class entertainment courtesy of ENSA, the UK Theatre/Entertainments Organisation. Solomon, the celebrated pianist, played there for nearly two hours one Sunday evening and to top it all off, he responded to audience requests, an almost unbelievable turn of events. He stopped playing only when the requests stopped.

Food was good, there was plenty to drink and we were looked after well by domestic staff who were refugees from the Baltic States. We almost ended up as a family.

I was allowed a second period of leave in the United Kingdom in August 1945 and I again spent this with my family at Shirebrook. One of my abiding memories of this leave was connected with the journey from Hamburg to the Hook of Holland. The train was a British Army of the Rhine Special, so a majority of the passengers were men (and women) who had seen service during the campaign through Europe. The journey across Germany was relatively uneventful, but problems began when the train slowed down at the frontier crossing point from Germany into Holland, and at other intervals on the way across the Netherlands to the Hook. As the train slowed, almost as if my magic, Dutch children by the dozen would appear alongside the railway track begging for food.

Formal meals were not available on the train, but at the Aitona railway station in Hamburg we had been provided with packed lunches in picnic-type boxes, and the standard was very good. The moment the children appeared, the train windows went down and the boxes were thrown out. The children were obviously desperate and the risks they were tempted to take were such that mounted Dutch policemen would ride alongside the train driving them away from the moving carriages. Nevertheless, the children carried on begging.

There were, perhaps a thousand service men and women on the train, and I estimated that at least five hundred boxes of food were thrown out, probably more. Sad to relate, a number of children were killed when the risks they took were too great.

Other occurrences inside the train helped to pass the time. We were usually sitting six to a table in an open carriage and it was only a matter of time before the occupants began displaying various goods they were taking back to the UK. I saw everything from cameras to diamonds and as I walked the length of the train; a substantial number of servicemen seemed to be displaying merchandise. There was a fair amount of evidence that the 'spoils of war' were on view and were on their way home to the United Kingdom.

I had a pleasant, relaxed leave with my family in the UK and my return to Niebull was fairly uneventful.

During the next few months we experienced little unpleasantness or hostility in doing our work and I was particularly pleased at one stage that I managed to acquire a BMW Sports car that had reputedly been built especially for Dr Ley, one of Hitler's ministers. I learned about the car's existence from an Informer who directed me to a local farmstead. After some fairly rigorous questioning, the farmer led me to a haystack under part of which was hidden the BMW car.

It still had some petrol in the tank, the engine sprang to life, so I drove it back to our base. I managed to hang on to the vehicle for some weeks and it really was a joy. Eventually, however, the Authorities forced me to hand it over, as it was not part of my official RAF inventory. I then downgraded myself to a clapped-out ten horsepower Opel saloon car that nobody seemed particularly interested in.

One special deviation from routine occurred when we were ordered to travel to a Luftwaffe base close to the Port of Esbjerg on the North Sea coast of Denmark. Our responsibility there was to ensure that the Germans did not sabotage the Radar installations. There were a sizeable number of Luftwaffe personnel on the Station and the attitude of some of them when we arrived was fairly hostile.

In particular, a group of young pilots strutted about the place as though they were still on active service and the Commanding Officer, an Oberst (Colonel) was quite aggressive. I therefore took steps to restrict the movement of the pilots and I gave the CO a forceful reminder that his war was over and that he was a prisoner of the Allies.

We also decided to take steps to remove three of the senior ranking pilots from the station for the best part of a morning.

We began this by walking into the rest room at their mess and singling out the three on the basis of, "You, you and you, outside, quickly!" We piled the three into the back of a truck and closed the canvas top so that they could not see what was happening. We said nothing to them and left them to ponder what we might be going to do with them.

Whilst carrying out various security checks on the site, we drove them around for the best part of the morning and then returned them to their quarters. They seemed a good deal less confident when we released them. Elementary though it all was, for the rest of our time there, they got on their feet pretty quickly whenever we put in an appearance, and we finished up well in control of the situation.

We spent several days on the airfield and on a given day a squadron of RAF bombers came out from the UK for the purpose, we were told, of testing the Radar System. This journey into Denmark was very much a one-off situation and we returned to our Niebull base after the fly-over had taken place.

Denmark after the desolation of Germany was like a picture-book kingdom. The streets and roads were beautifully clean, the roadsides were manicured and the buildings were in excellent decorative order. The people were friendly, there was food of all kinds, and travelling through the country was indeed a pleasure. Nearly everyone we met spoke some English. Our Assistant Provost Marshal joined us and entertained us quite regally one evening at the Central Hotel, Esbjerg. Wine, dining and music were indeed a welcome change. The job done we were reluctant to leave Denmark.

During the second half of 1945, life for the civilian population in Kreis Sud-Tondern began to improve and even though we were still the enemy, we experienced very little resentment at our presence.

The feeling among most of the population was that the war had done nothing for them and, indeed, in many cases they had suffered the loss of friends, relations and property.

The British were not regarded by the Germans as oppressive in their general attitude and the people seemed to want to get back to living in peace with their families. They had learned a bitter lesson and were looking to the future.

The period of strict non-fraternisation with the Germans ended after a year. The local Council Officers began to function again but we kept their activities under surveillance as one of our main duties.

By the turn of the year, the number of arrests had dropped almost to zero, and our duties became little more than a general surveillance operation.

Christmas and New Year, 1945/46 were pleasant occasions spent at our base in the typical British manner.

83 Group Police Unit
B.A.F.O.
Royal Air Force,
c/o B.A.O.R.

10th January 1946.

Dear Hallam

I had hoped to come to see you before leaving the Unit, but it is now obvious that I shall not be able to do so. I must therefore put in writing what I should have wished to say to you and the other NCOs of your Section.

My period of service with this Unit - despite its ups and downs has been the happiest part of my R.A.F. career. This has been due in large measure to the whole-hearted co-operation and unswerving loyalty which I have always enjoyed from all my NCOs. Your Section had to fend for itself and I was not able to give you the help you should have had, and you therefore deserve the greater credit that you have done such a very good job yourselves. You, in particular, have organised and administered the Section to my entire satisfaction, and both at 8 Corps District headquarters (G.b.I.(b).) and from the 12 Area Security Officer I have heard only favourable comments on the work of I\TO 6 R.A.F. Security Section.

In saying goodbye, I wish to thank you and all the personnel of your Section for your very worthy service, and to wish you the best of luck in whatever may be your future careers. If at any time I can be of assistance to any of you, please do not hesitate to write to me.

Will you please communicate the contents of this letter to all the NCOs, including the Sylt detachment.

Yours

Squadron Leader,
Assistant Provost Marshal, Security.

Valedictory message to the Author from his Commanding Officer.

Demobilisation of all the Armed Services began to take real effect in 1946 and I gradually lost members of the Team when their time for release came round. Replacements were not really called for as our main task had been completed. My own demobilisation was agreed for the 30th July 1946 and after more than five years on Active Service I began to look forward to getting out. I was asked to stay on and the offer of a long term Commission in the RAF made me think about signing-on and becoming a 'regular'.

However, I took demobilisation when my time came, and I returned to my home in England for a period of rest and relaxation. I thoroughly enjoyed helping my Father with his huge vegetable garden.

I rapidly went through the modest gratuity I was given on discharge from the RAF so I applied to the Foreign Office for a position and after a series of interviews I accepted a post as an Intelligence Officer in a grade equivalent to Captain. I returned to Germany where I carried out counter-espionage duties on the Staff of one of the Regional Intelligence Officers.

And there begins another story!

The author, posing with the Opel motor car requisitioned for use in occupied Germany.

NOBODY'S HERO

Author's Postscript

Trying to realistically describe what war is like to those who have not been directly involved is almost impossible. Besides, for every member of the Armed Forces the experience was different.

Looking back over the years, I am convinced that the balance between the things that went according to plan and those that did not was just about equal. However much training and preparation went in beforehand, the reality was always different in one way or another.

The task of organising defensive and offensive military operations involving millions of men and women some of whom were volunteers and the bulk of whom were conscripts, was complex in the extreme. People in the mass do not take kindly to violence, so the job of getting them trained and into the right place with the right equipment at the right time, with killing and destruction in mind, was never easy.

For the individual, the overriding consideration was the sheer impossibility of overcoming the fear of being killed. Life to most people is precious and trying to instil into them the need to kill or destroy was so often an insurmountable obstacle.

As regards my own personal feelings and reactions, I readily admit that I was afraid some of the time, but I fought a battle within myself to prevent those for whom I was responsible from registering the fact that I was afraid. I think, in my own defence, I may say that I succeeded, though I was aware that close colleagues who were with me on the battlefield shared deep down my feelings and anxieties. As often as not we were dependent upon each other for our survival.

Throughout my early life I always harboured strong views about cowardice, but I am now prepared to accept that some people did not have what it took to cope with the strains inherent in armed combat that might result in killing. I suppose it is a human problem that will continue to manifest itself as long as the human race exists.

The simple fact of being separated from family and friends was probably the greatest deprivation we suffered, particularly as periods of absence of four, five and six years applied in many, many cases.

War is a senseless, barbaric way of resolving problems. I therefore hope and trust that in putting my experience on paper I shall not be judged guilty of glorifying armed combat; that to me would constitute total failure. That is one reason why I have waited fifty years.

An abiding personal disappointment concerns the way in which military service was recognised by those in authority.

I was a Volunteer and five of the best years of my life, 21 to 26, were taken up in the service of the Crown. The pay I received was a pittance. The Government's way of acknowledging this was to send me, 18 months after the armistice, a cardboard package containing my service and campaign medals. Accompanying the medals was a small unsigned slip addressed to and from nobody. The external label on the package did not even refer to me as 'Mister'.

Perhaps, then, it would be fair to assume that nothing has really changed since Rudyard Kipling wrote his famous First World War ballad as a tribute to 'Tommy Atkins', the mythical and much abused soldier.

> *Tommy this, an' Tommy that,*
> *an' chuck him out, the brute.*
> *But it's Saviour of his Country,*
> *when the guns begin to shoot...*